THE STATISTICS COACH

THE STATISTICS
COACH Learning Through Practice

Lance W. Roberts
Karen Kampen
Tracey Peter

OXFORD
UNIVERSITY PRESS

OXFORD
UNIVERSITY PRESS

8 Sampson Mews, Suite 204, Don Mills, Ontario M3C 0H5
www.oupcanada.com

Oxford University Press is a department of the University of Oxford.
It furthers the University's objective of excellence in research, scholarship,
and education by publishing worldwide in

Oxford   New York
Auckland   Cape Town   Dar es Salaam   Hong Kong   Karachi
Kuala Lumpur   Madrid   Melbourne   Mexico City   Nairobi
New Delhi   Shanghai   Taipei   Toronto

With offices in
Argentina   Austria   Brazil   Chile   Czech Republic   France   Greece
Guatemala   Hungary   Italy   Japan   Poland   Portugal   Singapore
South Korea   Switzerland   Thailand   Turkey   Ukraine   Vietnam

Oxford is a trade mark of Oxford University Press
in the UK and in certain other countries

Published in Canada
by Oxford University Press

Library and Archives Canada Cataloguing in Publication

Roberts, Lance W., 1950-
The statistics coach : learning through practice / Lance
W. Roberts, Karen Kampen, Tracey Peter.

Includes index.
ISBN 978-0-19-542659-5

1. Social sciences—Statistical methods—Textbooks.
I. Kampen, Karen II. Peter, Tracey, 1973– III. Title.

HA29.R62 2010   300.1'5195   C2009-907240-8

Cover image: Cultura Photography/Veer

Contents

'You Play the Way You Practise': A Preface for Students

Most undergraduate students in sociology and other social science disciplines are required to take courses in both research methods and statistical analysis. Sometimes this content is covered in one course; more commonly, separate courses are devoted to each subject.

There are many good books on the market that cover the fundamentals of research methods and/or social statistics. The experience of our students indicates that as good as the available books are, they are deficient. Their deficiency relates to the kind of learning they encourage.

There are many ways we can learn things. These levels of learning are captured by different educational objectives. To get a sense of this range, think about the remarkable difference between being able to name the title and author of a novel (i.e., knowing simple facts) and being able to competently critique the author's work.

Using a standard taxonomy of educational objectives, most available research methods and social statistics books are focused on information and understanding—knowing the facts and learning the principles. This is fine as far as it goes, but it is limited. A further step on the learning progression involves being able to *apply* the facts and principles in realistic situations.

This book intends to advance this application objective. Like its companion volume, *The Methods Coach: Learning Through Practice*, this one seeks to advance your knowledge of several fundamental social statistics techniques by allowing you to practise.

The Importance of Practice

Athletic coaches drill their players with the dictum 'You play the way you practice.' This aphorism applies to all endeavours in which 'knowing' and 'doing' must be bridged. It is one thing to 'talk a good game', quite another to master the challenges of performance. In connecting knowing with doing, practice is the key—whether in sports, in the kitchen, or in the classroom.

This book aims at giving you the opportunity to 'practise' several of the fundamental concepts and principles you are learning in your social statistics course. Contrary to popular belief, practice does *not* make perfect. What practice does is *habituate*. If you repeatedly swing a golf club incorrectly or overcook your pasta, then you will surely habituate these performance deficiencies.

Learning through Coaching

For practice to be useful in improving your performance, it is best to have a 'coach'. For learning purposes, the role of a coach has two important components, one of which occurs prior to practice and the other after practice.

Prior to practice, a coach needs to *raise your awareness* of critical performance features. In the case of the golf swing, this might include noting your grip, club take-away, or position at the top of the swing. In the case of pasta preparation, it might mean the temperature of the water, ingredients added to it, or cooking time. In all cases, raising your awareness alerts you to key things to keep in mind when you practise.

After you have performed, the coach plays a second key role. This role is to *provide you with constructive feedback*. The goal of feedback is to let you see how you have performed compared to a preferred standard. You thought your golf swing was slow and smooth, but you are told that it was actually quick and jerky. You thought you put enough oil in the water and took the pasta out in time, but you did neither—which resulted in a sticky mass of starch.

In short, an optimal performance learning strategy involves three components. First, you are alerted to the key requirements of the skill. Second, you make the effort to perform the skill. Finally, you receive constructive feedback about your performance.

The Model

The Statistics Coach is based on this three-component 'coaching' model. The model is implemented in the form of 'labs' familiar to students in the natural sciences like chemistry and biology. The lab is a place of practice that is preceded by a 'demonstration' (which alerts students to key performance features) and is followed by 'feedback' (on the lab reports submitted by students).

The book contains 12 methods labs. Each lab consists of three parts: a 'tune-up', a 'lab application', and 'constructive feedback'. These three parts are intended to work as follows:

The Tune-up: Each module begins with a tune-up providing a succinct overview of the central statistical concepts that are the focus of the lab. The purpose of this component is to review and highlight core concepts under consideration.

The Lab Application: After the tune-up has focused your thinking, the lab gives you an opportunity to solidify your understanding of the core concepts through application. Each lab seeks for 'realism' by providing you with challenges that are similar to those faced by practising social researchers.

Constructive Feedback: The first two steps of each lab clarify core concepts and give you guided opportunities to put these ideas into practice. The final step involves feedback. Immediate, constructive feedback is necessary for reinforcement and remediation. You will find feedback regarding each lab application in the 'answers' available on an Oxford University Press website associated with this book [www.oupcanada.com/Statistics].

What's Covered

This book is not intended to replace the textbook used in your course. Rather, it supplements your textbook and will help to solidify your understanding of key statistical concepts and principles through guided application.

Any good-quality social statistics text covers a much larger range of topics than those on which this book focuses. Of necessity, your textbook provides an overview of many topics, while the 12 labs in this volume focus on key statistical concepts and principles. The goal is to move you from the basic understanding your textbook supplies to a more thorough understanding informed through practice.

The methods labs cover the following key topics:

Lab 1: An introduction to SPSS
Lab 2: Basic univariate analyses
Lab 3: The shape of distributions and z-scores
Lab 4: Data transformation
Lab 5: Bivariate tables
Lab 6: Trivariate tables
Lab 7: PRE measures for crosstabs
Lab 8: Correlation and regression
Lab 9: Inference and chi-square
Lab 10: Inference and t-tests
Lab 11: Samples and inferences
Lab 12: Putting it all together

Data Analysis

In order to practise these statistical analysis techniques, the labs utilize a variety of different data sets. Many of these data sets are Canadian, but others include the World Values Survey, a data set on National Hockey League players, and a sample of South Africans. So there is a wide variety of interesting content in the mix.

To help you analyze the data sets, the book provides you with focused instruction on how to use SPSS analysis software.

Developing Confidence

Genuine self-confidence and self-esteem[1] are precious (perhaps the *most* precious) human commodities. Authentic self-confidence and associated self-esteem derive from the *mastery* of something *worthwhile* and *difficult*. This is why these precious commodities are not awarded for incompetence (vs. mastery), frivolousness (vs. worthiness), or simplicity (vs. difficulty).

For this reason, we hope that you will find many of the ideas and applications in this book challenging. If you do, this is a positive sign. If you do not move out of your comfort zone, you will not grow.

Learning is different from certification. Learning involves change, and change inevitably involves making errors. So don't be afraid to make mistakes. And just as important, don't be discouraged by your mistakes.

We encourage you to study the tune-up points carefully and put forward your best effort in each lab application. After you have completed the application, consult the feedback information on the Oxford University Press website associated with this book [www.oupcanada.com/Statistics]. Each time you do so, you will learn something—either that you can successfully put the statistical techniques into practice or that your skills need refinement. When you learn the former lesson, your confidence will deservedly grow. When the latter is the lesson learned, it should motivate you to return to the core ideas and continue your informed practice. The path to success and confidence is through successive approximations.

Feedback

Our students have benefited extensively from each of the lab applications presented in this book. However, we are practitioners of what we preach and are certain that improvements can be made. If you would like to share your experiences in working through the labs or have constructive suggestions for improvement, please send them along to Lance_Roberts@umanitoba.ca.

We trust you will learn as much from consuming these applications as we have from producing them.

Lance W. Roberts
Karen Kampen
Tracey Peter

LAB 1
An Introduction to SPSS

▶ Tune-up

The labs in this book all use the software package SPSS for analyzing data. SPSS, which stands for Statistical Package for the Social Sciences, is one of the most commonly used analysis packages.

In order to use SPSS to analyze quantitative data, you need to become familiar with the essentials of the program. This lab familiarizes you with these program 'basics', including how to open and close the software, access data files, define new variables, and enter data.

You will find the 'SPSS Essentials' for all of the labs right after Lab 12. For this lab you need to read and familiarize yourself with Section 1 of SPSS Essentials. You should read Section 1 and then consult it again as you work your way through Application 1.

LAB 1 APPLICATION

Learning Objectives

The following lab questions are directed at helping you translate the material in Section 1 of SPSS Essentials into concrete research situations. Specifically, this lab assignment challenges you to clarify your understanding of:

- The basic components and operations of SPSS
- How to define variables
- How to enter data

Most of the statistical analysis exercises in this book use existing survey data. These data are referred to as 'secondary data' because they were collected by someone else for their own research purposes. However, researchers often collect their own ('primary') data. This lab teaches you how to set up and enter primary data in the SPSS program and access secondary data.

The original data in this lab will come from your responses to a brief questionnaire. After collecting the data, you will learn how to set up SPSS so that the responses can be entered into the program in a format that makes them easy to analyze.

With your data defined and entered, the lab then directs you to a set of additional cases that you can add to your data set.

Part 1: The survey questionnaire

Instructions

Imagine that you are part of a research study that requires you to respond to a survey questionnaire. The questions are listed below. Assume that there is no interviewer present. Just fill the questions out as you would if you were participating in an actual self-administered survey. Like most questionnaires, the survey does not provide you with a detailed description of the researcher's hypotheses or theoretical approach. These issues will be introduced in the next lab when you analyze the SPSS data set of survey responses.

Now take a few minutes and complete the following survey questionnaire.

The following questions concern aspects of your personality. For each question, circle a number from 1 ('disagree completely') to 7 ('agree completely').

1. Whenever I'm faced with a choice, I try to imagine what all the other possibilities are, even ones that aren't present at the moment.	1	2	3	4	5	6	7
2. No matter how satisfied I am with my job, it's only right for me to be on the lookout for better opportunities.	1	2	3	4	5	6	7
3. When I'm in the car listening to the radio, I often check other stations to see if something better is playing, even if I'm relatively satisfied with what I'm listening to.	1	2	3	4	5	6	7
4. When I watch TV, I channel-surf, often scanning through the available options even while attempting to watch one program.	1	2	3	4	5	6	7
5. I treat relationships like clothing; I expect to try a lot on before finding the perfect fit.	1	2	3	4	5	6	7
6. I often find it difficult to shop for a gift for a friend.	1	2	3	4	5	6	7
7. Renting videos is really difficult. I'm always struggling to pick the best one.	1	2	3	4	5	6	7
8. When shopping, I have a hard time finding clothing that I really love.	1	2	3	4	5	6	7
9. I'm a big fan of lists that attempt to rank things (the best movies, the best singers, the best athletes, the best novels, etc.).	1	2	3	4	5	6	7
10. I find that writing is very difficult, even if it's just writing a letter to a friend, because it's so hard to word things just right. I often do several drafts even of simple things.	1	2	3	4	5	6	7
11. No matter what I do, I have the highest standards for myself.	1	2	3	4	5	6	7
12. I never settle for second-best.	1	2	3	4	5	6	7
13. I often fantasize about living in ways that are quite different from my actual life.	1	2	3	4	5	6	7
14. Once I make a decision, I don't look back.	1	2	3	4	5	6	7
15. Whenever I make a choice, I'm curious about what would have happened if I had chosen differently.	1	2	3	4	5	6	7
16. If I make a choice and it turns out well, I still feel like something of a failure if I find out that another choice would have turned out better.	1	2	3	4	5	6	7
17. Whenever I make a choice, I try to get information about how the other alternatives turned out.	1	2	3	4	5	6	7
18. When I think about how I'm doing in life, I often assess opportunities I have passed up.	1	2	3	4	5	6	7

Source: The American Psychological Association.

In addition, the survey also requires some background information, so please provide responses to the following additional questions:

What is your age group? (circle one)   1. Under 20

2. 20–24

3. 25–34

4. 35+

Are you male or female? (circle one)   1. Male

2. Female

During the past three months, on average about how many hours per week did you work

for pay? _____

Part 2: Defining the variables and entering the data

Defining variables

You have now completed the data collection for a research study with a sample size of one! But the process would be the same if you were in a large lecture hall where every one of the 250 students completed the same survey.

As described in Section 1 of SPSS Essentials, before you can analyze the data using SPSS, you need to enter the data and define each variable. To do this, you need to apply the techniques outlined in Section 1 of SPSS Essentials under the section 'Creating or Expanding a Data Matrix'.

To begin this process, you need to switch to the 'Variable View' in the Data Editor window. In this window, you need to follow the five-step process for *defining each* of the variables.

The survey contains 21 questions, and each of these questions is a variable. It is common to add a variable called 'identification number' (IDNUM) at the beginning of a data set, so *your completed data matrix should include 22 variables*.

Once you have finished defining the variables for each of the questions in the survey, you are ready to enter the data.

Entering data

So far, all the data you have are those you collected from yourself: a sample size of one. To enter these data into the matrix, you need to switch from 'Variable View' to 'Data View' in the Data Editor window. You should now see a matrix that has the same form as Figure 6 in SPSS Essentials (the content, of course, will be different).

In 'Data View', you now *enter your responses* to each of the survey questions. To do this, follow the steps just above Figure 6 in SPSS Essentials.

Congratulations! You have now created a complete (albeit very small) SPSS data set.

Expanding the data set

The work you have completed in defining the variables and entering the data is exactly how all data sets are created. The principal difference is that no realistic data set has only one case. In conventional circumstances, after you have entered the data for the first case, you would proceed to entering the data for the second case, the third, and so on until all cases in your sample (often more than 1000) are entered.

To demonstrate to yourself how this works, have two or three of your friends answer the same questions you did, record their answers, and then enter their responses into your data set. Each time you do this, you will notice that your sample size is growing.

As you can imagine, data entry quickly becomes tedious work. To spare you this tedium and help you to expand your sample to a slightly larger size, we are providing you with an additional 20 cases. You will find these cases on the website for this book (www.oupcanada.com/Statistics) under the SPSS data file name 'schwartz.sav'.

If you go to the website and open this file, you will see a large data matrix similar to the one you have created. The 22 variables are listed in the columns and arranged in the same order as the data set you created. Now all you need to do is *copy and paste* the data from the 'schwartz.sav' data file into your data file.

When you have completed this step, you should have a fully documented data set of at least 21 cases (depending on how many of your friends' responses you entered).

Saving the file

Now that your data set is complete, you need to save it for consultation in Lab 2. To save your data set, follow the instructions in the 'Saving Files' section in SPSS Essentials.

Part 3: Examining your work

Now that your data set is fully documented, you can either create a codebook for the entire data set or examine the codes for specific variables. To understand how each of these procedures works, you should do both.

Creating a codebook

Just above Figure 3 in SPSS Essentials is a section titled 'Creating a Full Codebook'. Follow the three steps listed there, and you will generate a codebook for your data set that is analogous to the one illustrated in Figure 3.

Note that when you ask SPSS to generate a codebook, it puts the results in a *separate window*—the Viewer or Output Window.

Codes for particular variables

The codebook reproduces the coding scheme for *all* the variables in the data set. But often you are only interested in the codes for a *specific* variable or set of variables. To get the coding for specific variables, follow the procedure listed in the SPSS Essentials section 'Examining Codes of a Specific Variable', just above Figure 4.

Follow this procedure for any variable in your data set, and you will get a display similar to the one portrayed in Figure 4.

Part 4: Closing up

When your SPSS work is completed, you need to save your work and exit the program. You will find the procedures for performing each of these tasks in the final two parts of Section 1 of SPSS Essentials.

Note that if you are doing a lot of analyses, it is wise to *save your work regularly* during your working session. Sooner or later, through accident or negligence, you will experience the frustration of having SPSS do something unintended. If you regularly save your work, you will minimize the consequences of such errors, reducing the backtracking you might have to do.

LAB 2
Basic Univariate Analyses

▶ Tune-up

This lab is about analyzing the scores of single variables, which is why the procedures are labelled *univariate* analysis. You can use the techniques to look at multiple variables, but univariate analysis considers the variables *one at a time*.

For this lab, you need to read and familiarize yourself with Section 2, 'Describing Distributions', in the SPSS Essentials materials at the end of the book. You should read through Section 2 and then consult these materials as you work your way through Application 2.

Creating new variables from existing ones

In Lab Application 1, you answered a series of survey questions and entered your responses into a data matrix. Then you increased the sample size of your project in two ways. First, you gathered and entered the survey responses of a few of your friends, and second, you transferred additional responses from a data set we provided.

The core of the survey in Lab 1 consisted of 18 'personality-type' questions. This set of questions was developed by Barry Schwartz, whose recent research has focused on the idea that modern Westerners have too much choice. Schwartz begins with the basic observation that modern life has become incredibly complex, posing us with an overwhelming array of choices: the perfect career, the perfect partner, or simply the perfect cellphone plan. He then argues that this complexity ultimately makes many of us less satisfied and less happy, and more tired, stressed, and depressed. Our expectations may have become so unrealistically high that we are never truly fulfilled.

Schwartz argues that certain 'types' of people are more prone to being overwhelmed by the endless choices offered in modern societies. The type that is more prone to this form of dissatisfaction is called a 'maximizer'. Maximizers are contrasted with the type called 'satisficers', who are less overwhelmed by choices. The following commentary elaborates on this distinction.

Maximizers are people whose general orientation to life is that 'only the best will do.' Schwartz gives an example on page 77 of his recent book *The Paradox of Choice* (2004)[1]:

Imagine going shopping for a sweater. You go to a couple of department stores or boutiques, and after an hour or so, you find a sweater that you like. The color is striking, the fit is flattering, and the wool feels soft against your skin. The sweater costs $89. You're all set to take it to the salesperson when you think about the store down the street that has a reputation for low prices. You take the sweater back to its display table, hide it under a pile of other sweaters of a different size (so that no one will buy it out from under you), and leave to check out the other store.

Satisficers, by contrast, are people who are willing to settle for what is 'good enough' without constantly worrying that there is something better out there:

> A satisficer has criteria and standards. She searches until she finds an item that meets those standards, and at that point, she stops. As soon as she finds a sweater that meets her standard of fit, quality, and price in the very first store she enters, she buys it—end of story. She is not concerned about better sweaters or better bargains just around the corner [Schwartz 2004, 78].

This appreciation of the distinction between maximizers and satisficers is abstract and conceptual. You will recall that researchers are interested in more than just thinking and talking about abstract concepts; they are interested in measuring them.[2]

Schwartz operationalizes the distinction between maximizers and satisficers by adding up each respondent's scores to Questions 1 through 13 on the survey presented in Lab 1. Based on these total scores, people are classified as follows:

Maximizers score	65 or more
Satisficers score	Under 40

Scores between 40 and 64 are mixed, ambiguous classifications.

Schwartz argues that the distinction between maximizers and satisficers is an important one because of its implications for mental and emotional well-being. For example, he makes the case that maximizers are more likely to be regretful, pessimistic, dissatisfied, and depressed.

Responses to Questions 14 through 18 on the Schwartz survey provide a means of computing one example of emotional condition, the 'regret scale'. The steps for calculating a respondent's 'regret score' include:

1. Adding up the scores for Questions 15 through 18.
2. For Question 14, *subtracting* the respondent's score from 8.
3. The sum of (1) and (2) is the regret score.

What the 'regret'; and the 'maximization' scores illustrate is the power of taking answers to specific questions and creating new variables with them.

Statistics

All statistics are 'summaries' in the sense that they take a large amount of data and distil it. Consider the following example: Imagine that 100 students in a class wrote a test last week. At the beginning of class, one student raises her hand and inquires, 'How did the class do on last week's test?' The professor replies '79, 38, 92, 63, 67, 81, 55, 49, 77, 64, etc. . . .' until he has recited 100 scores. This answer is correct, since each student's test score is presented. But the response is not very helpful, since the listeners will be overwhelmed and confused by the volume of information.

If the professor, instead, had responded with a statistic summarizing the class results, the answer would have been helpful. The response 'The class average is 68 per cent' would have been satisfactory. In this case, one statistic (average = 68%) provides an understandable summary of how the entire class performed.

Types of univariate statistics

Univariate statistics provide summaries of single variables. Remember that variables are properties of objects that can differ or change. So, for example, social class and ethnicity are variables because when we measure these properties in a sample of people, different people give different answers. Some have higher social classes, some lower. Some are Ukrainians, others Nigerians, still others Peruvians.

When we use statistics to summarize a set of responses to a variable, there are only two kinds of things to be summarized. Hence, there are two kinds of univariate statistics.

One kind of univariate statistic is called 'measures of central tendency'. Central tendency refers to where the scores tend to 'cluster' or 'converge' on a variable. It is where the 'centre' is, where 'most' or 'typical' scores are. In the class test scores just mentioned, the 'central tendency' is the test score that students typically received.

Measures of central tendency are all forms of 'average', and there are three of them, including mode, median, and mean. How these statistics are calculated is not a topic considered here. However, it is worthwhile reviewing the meaning of each of these measures of central tendency, since these meanings affect each statistic's interpretation.

The *mode* is the score on a variable that occurs most frequently. Hence, the interpretation of the mode takes the form: 'The most frequently occurring score on the variable _____ is _____.'

The *median* is the score that is in the middle of a rank-ordered distribution. The interpretation of the median takes the following form: '_____ is the score that has half of the cases above it and half below.'

The *mean* is the score that everyone would receive *if all cases in the sample had the same score*. As you can see, the mean is hypothetical in the sense that it assumes perfect equality (i.e., every case having the same score). Hence, interpretation of the mean takes the form: 'If all cases had the same score, that score would be _____.'

Beyond knowing where scores on a variable tend to cluster (i.e., measure of central tendency), the only other feature that can be summarized is how spread out the scores are. Statistics that summarize this variability are called measures of dispersion.

There are specific statistics that measure dispersion, including the range, index of qualitative variation, standard deviation, and variance. For purposes of this lab, it is not necessary to review either the calculation or interpretation of measures of dispersion.

Selecting univariate statistics

Not all measures of central tendency and dispersion are appropriate for every variable. The appropriateness of specific univariate statistics depends on the level of measurement of the variable.[3]

Table 2.1 displays the appropriate central tendency and dispersion measures for various levels of measurement. In this table, the statistic in italics is the most commonly used for a specific level of measurement.

Table 2.1

Level of measurement	Measure(s) of central tendency	Measure(s) of dispersion[4]
Nominal	*Mode*	n/a
Ordinal	Mode, *Median*	*Range*
Interval	Mode, Median, *Mean**	Range, Variance, *Standard Deviation*
Ratio	Mode, Median, *Mean**	Range, Variance, *Standard Deviation*

* Except if you have problems with outliers (extreme values), in which case use medians.

LAB 2 APPLICATION

Learning Objectives

The following lab questions are directed at helping you translate the material in this lab and Section 2 of SPSS Essentials into concrete research situations. Specifically, this lab assignment challenges you to clarify your understanding of:

- How to generate and interpret frequency distributions
- How to create basic graphs
- How to recognize and connect levels of measurement to statistics
- How to interpret various measures of central tendency and dispersion

Data requirements

To conduct the analysis for this application, go to the website and download the data set 'schwartz198.sav'. This data set includes 198 cases for all the variables included in the survey discussed in Lab 1. The variables in this data set are fully defined, using the same procedures you used in Lab 1. Note, however, that the variables may have slightly different names from those you chose for your data set. But such labelling is a cosmetic matter that makes no substantive difference.

In addition to the variables you are familiar with from Lab 1, the data set for this lab contains two additional variables, labelled 'maxscale' and 'regrets'. The 'maxscale' variable is the score discussed in the Tune-up that allow you to view 'maximizers' and 'satisficers'. 'Maxscale' is computed from the answers to Questions 1 through 13. The 'regrets' variable is the computation of the 'regret scores' discussed in the Tune-Up and is based on computations using survey variables 14 through 18.

Part 1: Frequency distributions and graphs

Frequency distributions and graphs provide a basic understanding of the evidence before any statistical analyses are conducted. Complete the following steps to get a sense of several variables in the data set:

1. Run frequency distributions for the variables 'maxscale', 'gender', and 'agegroup'. Examine the output carefully to get an initial look at the distributions.

2. Using your output, fill in the blanks for the following statement:

In this sample of 198 respondents, _____% of respondents were clear maximizers (i.e., scored 65 or above on the scale), while _____% were clear satisficers (scoring below 40), and the remaining _____% fell somewhere in between these extremes. The sample was comprised of _____% men and _____% women. _____% of the respondents were under 25 years of age, while _____% were aged between 25 and 34 and _____% were aged 35 or older.

3. What number of cases (n) corresponds with each of your percentages in question 2?

Maximizers: _____ Satisficers: _____ In between: _____

Men: _____ Women: _____

Under age 25: _____ Age 25–34: _____ Age 35 or older: _____

4. Charts and graphs are another means of viewing distributions. Produce the specified graphs for each of the following variables:

'sex':   Bar graph
'agegroup':   Pie chart
'workhrs':   Histogram

Part 2: Measures of central tendency and dispersion

1. Selecting appropriate statistics requires correctly identifying the level of measurement of the variables involved. Table 2.2 identifies several variables on the survey used in the first lab and this one. In the space beside each variable, *identify the level of measurement of the variable* in the data set. (It might be helpful to consult the survey questionnaire provided in Lab 1.)

Table 2.2

Variable	Level of measurement
'gender'	
'agegroup'	
'workhrs'	
Q1	
Q10	
Q15	
'maxscale'	
'regrets'	

2. For each of the eight variables identified in the previous section, run both frequency distributions and *appropriate* measures of central tendency and dispersion.

   Based on your analysis output, complete Table 2.3 by writing in the values of the *appropriate* measures of central tendency and dispersion for each variable. Leave the boxes blank where the statistic is inappropriate. Round your answers to the nearest decimal place (e.g., 10.256 = 10.3).

Table 2.3

Variable	Mean	Median	Mode	Standard deviation	Variance	Range
'gender'						
'agegroup'						
'workhrs'						
Q1						
Q10						
Q15						
'maxscale'						
'regrets'						

3. In the spaces below, provide an interpretation of the statistics you have generated.

Central tendency measure for 'workhrs':

_____

_____

Central tendency measure for 'gender':

_____

_____

Central tendency measure for Q15:

_____

_____

Dispersion measure for Q10:

_____

_____

LAB 3
The Shape of Distributions and Z-Scores

◗ Tune-up

In the last lab, you learned about two central properties of any univariate (i.e., single variable) distribution. These properties included identifying (1) what a 'typical' or 'average' score on the variable was (central tendency) and (2) how spread out from the centre scores on the variable were (dispersion). Various statistics provide means of summarizing the data on a variable in terms of these two properties.

This lab concentrates on some additional features of univariate distributions—including their shape and concentration of scores.

Shape of distributions

In Lab 2 you learned how to create graphs. Graphs simply take the information from a frequency distribution and display it in 'picture' (i.e., graphic) form. Examining a graph lets you see the shape of a distribution.

The shape of a univariate distribution is characterized by three features, including modality, symmetry, and kurtosis. Let's review each of these characteristics.

Modality refers to how many modes the distribution has. Recall that the mode is a measure of central tendency that identifies the most frequently occurring attribute(s) of a variable. In univariate graphs, the attributes of the variable are identified on the horizontal axis, while the frequency (or percentage) of cases is identified on the vertical axis. This means that on a graph, the 'mode' is evident by the number of 'humps' a distribution has. Hence, a distribution can be unimodal (one 'hump'), bimodal (two 'humps'), and so on.

Technically, the mode is the value that occurs most frequently. However, in describing the shape of distributions, this definition is relaxed slightly. In practice, distributions are called 'bimodal', for example, even if the second 'hump' is somewhat lower than the highest one.

The graphs in Figure 3.1 illustrate unimodal and bimodal distributions.

Figure 3.1 Unimodal and bimodal distributions

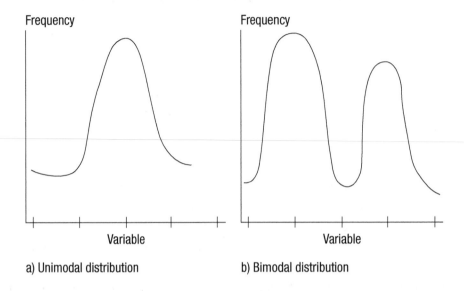

a) Unimodal distribution   b) Bimodal distribution

The second feature characterizing distributions is the degree of *symmetry*. Distributions are symmetrical if, around the centre, the halves of the distributions are mirror images. Figure 3.2 illustrates symmetrical distribution.

Figure 3.2 Symmetrical distribution

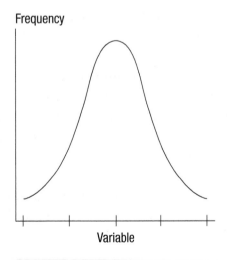

Symmetrical distribution

As the shape of a distribution deviates from symmetry, it becomes more 'skewed'. Although there are statistics that can compute the precise level of 'skewedness', conceptually, distributions can be 'negatively' or 'positively' skewed.

Distributions with a negative skew are those in which the 'tail' of the left-hand side of the distribution is longer than that of the right. Positively skewed distributions have a longer right-hand tail of the distribution. Examples of each type appear in Figure 3.3.

Figure 3.3 Negatively and positively skewed distributions

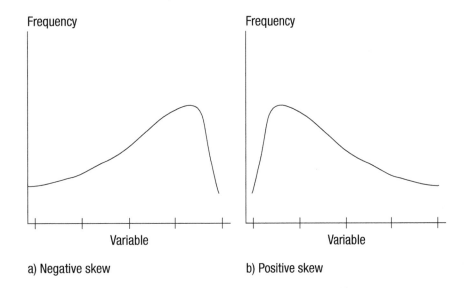

a) Negative skew   b) Positive skew

The third distinguishing characteristic of distributions is their level of *kurtosis*. Look at the two distributions in Figure 3.4. They are the same in terms of their modality (unimodal), and both are symmetrical. But the shape of these distributions is not the same. Their difference is captured by kurtosis, which refers to how 'peaked' a distribution is.

Figure 3.4 Level of kurtosis in a distribution

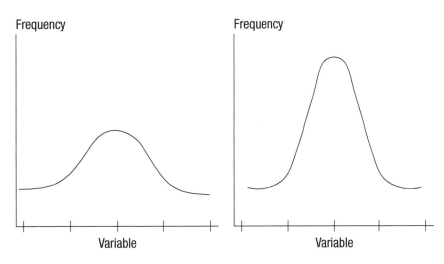

Level of kurtosis in a distribution

As with skewedness, there are precise statistics for calculating kurtosis. However, the basic ideas are captured in the following terms. Distributions that are very 'peaked' are called 'leptokurtic'; those that are flat are called 'platokurtic', and those in between are called 'mesokurtic'. Examples of each type appear in Figure 3.5.

Figure 3.5 Leptokurtic, platokurtic, and mesokurtic distributions

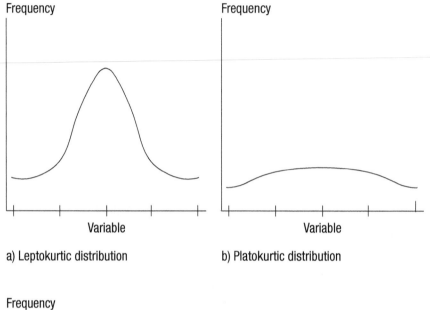

a) Leptokurtic distribution

b) Platokurtic distribution

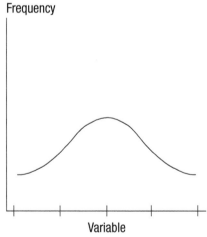

c) Mesokurtic distribution

The normal curve

The classic 'normal' curve is simply a graph of a univariate distribution that has three special characteristics. These characteristics concern modality, symmetry, and the connection between central tendency and dispersion. Let's consider these characteristics in turn.

A normal curve is a unimodal distribution in which *all three measures of central tendency (mode, median, and mean) are the same* (or, in practice, about the same).

Second, a normal curve is a symmetrical distribution, which means that the halves are mirror images of one another. (Again, in practice, the 'more-or-less so' provision applies.)

The final feature of normal curves is the most powerful (and wonderful). To appreciate this wonderfulness requires a bit of review. Remember that univariate distributions are characterized by statistics that measure central tendency and dispersion. Since the normal curve features apply to variables at higher (i.e., interval and ratio) levels of measurement, they can be characterized by the mean (for central tendency) and the standard deviation (for dispersion).

Take, for example, two different variables, such as 'peanut butter consumption' (in spoonfuls) and 'errors made on the last research methods test' (a specific number). For a sample of 500 students, their peanut butter consumption will have a specific mean and standard deviation (e.g., mean, 8; standard deviation, 2.3). Likewise, this sample of students' 'test errors' will have a specific mean and standard deviation (e.g., mean, 18, standard deviation, 6.1). So far, this is just a review of what you know.

But given this background, you are in a position to appreciate the third, powerful feature of normal curves, which is that *every normal curve has a fixed relationship between the mean (measuring central tendency) and standard deviation (measuring dispersion)*. This feature deserves some elaboration. The inclusion of the word 'every' denotes that this same connection between mean and standard deviation exists *independent of the variable being measured*. In other words, this rule applies for 'peanut butter consumption' as well as for 'test errors'. The 'fixed relationship' feature means that for every normally distributed variable, when you *begin at the mean* and go out a *fixed distance*, you find the *same percentage of cases*. Some common benchmarks of this 'fixed relationship' include the following:

- Mean ± one standard deviation = 68 per cent of cases
- Mean ± two standard deviations = 95 per cent of cases
- Mean ± three standard deviations = 99 per cent of cases

Applying these benchmarks to our example means that 68 per cent of students consume between 5.7 and 10.3 spoonfuls of peanut butter (8 ± 2.3), and 68 per cent of students made between 11.9 and 24.1 errors (18 ± 6.1) on the last research methods test.

Standard scores

The fixed relationship between means and standard deviations of normally distributed variables permits powerful comparisons. Perhaps you have heard the colloquial expression 'you cannot compare apples and oranges.' This expression makes the point that when two 'things' are different, comparison is problematic. In research terms, the 'things' being compared are variables, and comparisons are problematic because the variables are measured in different units. In our example, 'peanut butter consumption' is measured in 'spoonfuls', while 'test errors' is measured in terms of 'number of mistakes'. Spoonfuls of peanut butter and test mistakes are clearly not the same thing.

It turns out, however, that you can compare different things. The trick is to convert them to a *common base*. For example, since apples and oranges are both fruits, they are comparable in terms of their 'fruitiness' (setting aside, of course, the separate issue of how to actually measure 'fruitiness').

Similarly, it is possible to compare peanut butter consumption and test errors *or any other variables that are normally distributed*. The 'common base' required of such comparisons comes from the fact that all normally distributed variables have the same relationship between mean and standard deviation.

Using this principle, when variables are converted to a common base, they move from being in their original units (e.g., spoonfuls of peanut butter, numbers of mistakes) to a common unit. This common unit is *standard deviation units*, and the results are called 'standard scores'. Standard scores are also called 'z-scores'.

This manual is not intended to show you how standard scores are calculated. For current purposes, SPSS can do it for you.

Interpreting z-scores

The z-score for a particular value of a variable tells you how many standard deviation units away from the mean that individual's score is. For example, if my peanut butter consumption has a z-score of +1.74, this means that my score is 1.74 standard deviation units above the mean. If your test errors z-score is +0.66, it means that your mistakes are 0.66 standard deviation units above the mean. A graph of our relative scores is presented in Figure 3.6.

Figure 3.6 Z-scores

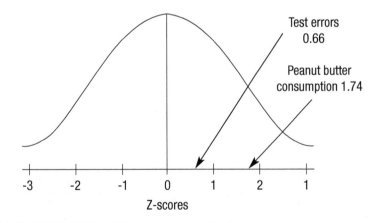

This graphic illustrates two important points. First, it shows that variables measured in different units (peanut butter consumption and test mistakes) are comparable as long as they are normally distributed. Second, the graph shows that my peanut butter consumption is more 'deviant' or 'extraordinary' (compared to the mean) than your test mistake rate.

There is another way to interpret standard scores that has more intuitive appeal. This method involves using a z-score table. The z-score table (an example is Table 3.2 at the end of this lab) is set up with the z-scores (to the first decimal place) listed in the left hand column (under 'z'). The row at the top of the table provides the 'second decimal place' of the z-score. So, for example, a z-score of 1.74 is found at the *intersection* of the 1.7 row and the .04 column. If you check this out, you should find the number 0.4591.

The numbers *inside* the z-score table can be interpreted as the *percentage* of the cases that fall *between the z-score and the mean.* For example, the z-score of +1.74 is my peanut butter consumption score in standard deviation units. When you look up 1.74 in the table, you see that 45.91 (i.e., 0.4591 x 100) per cent of cases fall between my peanut butter consumption score and the mean.

If you follow the same procedure for your (hypothetical) test error score, the z-score of +0.66 provides a table value of 0.2454. This means that 24.54 per cent of cases (0.2454 x 100) fall between your hypothetical score and the mean. Figure 3.7 presents these results in graphic form.

Figure 3.7

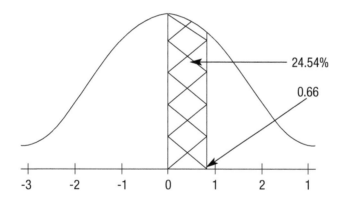

Given that normal curves are symmetrical, we can conclude that 95.91 per cent of persons consume less peanut butter than I do, and 74.54 per cent of persons make fewer methods test errors than you (hypothetically) do.

LAB 3 APPLICATION

Learning Objectives

The following lab questions are directed at helping you translate the material in this lab and Section 3 of SPSS Essentials into concrete research situations. Specifically, this lab assignment challenges you to clarify your understanding of:

- How to generate and interpret the shape of distributions
- How to generate and interpret standard scores for variables

Data requirements

To conduct the analysis for this application, go to the website and download the data set 'NHL2006.sav'. This data set includes various kinds of information on National Hockey League (NHL) players.

Part 1: Understanding the shape of distributions and the normal curve

Before examining statistics associated with the normal curve, we need to focus on the shape of distributions and their characteristics.

Instructions

1. Run frequency distributions for 'salary' (player's salary in $US) and 'weight' (player's weight in pounds). At the same time, request the mean and median and a histogram with a normal curve.

2. Examine each of your histograms carefully, paying attention to their overall shape. Look at your descriptive statistics. Imagine where you would mark the location of the mean and median on each histogram.

3. In the following chart, summarize the distributions of 'salary' and 'weight' by checking only those boxes that accurately describe your results:

Table 3.1

	Salary	Weight
Symmetrical curve		
Bell-shaped curve		
Mean and median coincide		
Approximately normal		
Positively skewed		
Negatively skewed		

Part 2: Using z-scores to solve problems

In the following exercise, you will use z-scores to compare specific NHL players with others in the NHL. To do so, you first need to convert each player's raw values into z-score values.

Instructions

1. Run a frequency distribution for 'height', requesting appropriate measures of central tendency and a histogram with a normal curve. Answer the following question:

   Do your results suggest that players' height is normally distributed? _____

   What evidence supports your conclusion?

   _____

2. Using the *Descriptives* procedure, create a new variable called 'Zheight' that converts each player's height into standard deviation units (i.e., z-scores).

3. In the Data Editor window, scroll down to the player Mats Sundin, who in this 2006 data base was with the Toronto Maple Leafs. What are his values for 'height' and 'Zheight'? (Please round to *two* decimal places here and in Question 4 below.)

   Height: _____ Zheight: _____

4. In the Data Editor window, scroll down to Markus Naslund, who in 2006 was playing for the Vancouver Canucks. What are his values for 'height' and 'Zheight'?

   Height: _____ Zheight: _____

5. Using the information that you gathered above, draw and label a standardized normal curve. Mark the approximate location where Sundin's and Naslund's z-scores will fall. Shade the area of the curve that lies in between the two z-scores.

6. Using the table of areas under the normal curve below, calculate the percentage of NHL players who are *shorter than* Sundin but *taller than* Naslund.

    Procedure:

    _____

    _____

    _____

    _____

    _____

    Result:

    _____: percentage of NHL players who are shorter than Sundin but taller than Naslund.

Table 3.2: Table of areas under the normal curve

z	.00	.01	.02	.03	.04	.05	.06	.07	.08	.09
0.0	.0000	.0040	.0080	.0120	.0160	.0190	.0239	.0279	.0319	.0359
0.1	.0398	.0438	.0478	.0517	.0557	.0596	.0636	.0675	.0714	.0753
0.2	.0793	.0832	.0871	.0910	.0948	.0987	.1026	.1064	.1103	.1141
0.3	.1179	.1217	.1255	.1293	.1331	.1368	.1406	.1443	.1480	.1517
0.4	.1554	.1591	.1628	.1664	.1700	.1736	.1772	.1808	.1844	.1879
0.5	.1915	.1950	.1985	.2019	.2054	.2088	.2123	.2157	.2190	.2224
0.6	.2257	.2291	.2324	.2357	.2389	.2422	.24.54	.2486	.2517	.2549
0.7	.2580	.2611	.2642	.2673	.2704	.2734	.2764	.2794	.2823	.2852
0.8	.2881	.2910	.2939	.2967	.2995	.3032	.3051	.3078	.3106	.3133
0.9	.3159	.3186	.3212	.3238	.3264	.3289	.3315	.3340	.3365	.3389
1.0	.3413	.3438	.3461	.3485	.3508	.3531	.3554	.3577	.3599	.3621
1.1	.3643	.3665	.3686	.3708	.3729	.3749	.3770	.3790	.3810	.3830
1.2	.3849	.3869	.3888	.3907	.3925	.3944	.3962	.3980	.3997	.4015
1.3	.4032	.4049	.4066	.4082	.4099	.4115	.4131	.4147	.4162	.4177
1.4	.4192	.4207	.4222	.4236	.4251	.4265	.4279	.4292	.4306	.4319
1.5	.4332	.4345	.4357	.4370	.4382	.4394	.4406	.4418	.4429	.4441
1.6	.4452	.4463	.4474	.4484	.4495	.4505	.4515	.4525	.4535	.4545
1.7	.4554	.4564	.4573	.4582	.4591	.4599	.4608	.4616	.4625	.4633
1.8	.4641	.4649	.4656	.4664	.4571	.4578	.4686	.4693	.4699	.4706
1.9	.4713	.4719	.4726	.4732	.4738	.4744	.4750	.4756	.4761	.4767
2.0	.4772	.4778	.4783	.4788	.4793	.4798	.4803	.4808	.4812	.4817
2.1	.4821	.4826	.4830	.4834	.4838	.4842	.4846	.4850	.5854	.4857
2.2	.4861	.4864	.4868	.4871	.4875	.4878	.4881	.4884	.4887	.4890
2.3	.4893	.4896	.4898	.4901	.4904	.4906	.4909	.4911	.4913	.4916
2.4	.4918	.4920	.4922	.4925	.4927	.4929	.4931	.4932	.4934	.4936
2.5	.4938	.4940	.4941	.4943	.4945	.4946	.4948	.4949	.4951	.4952
2.6	.4953	.4955	.4956	.4957	.4959	.4960	.4961	.4962	.4963	.4964
2.7	.4965	.4966	.4967	.4968	.4969	.4970	.4971	.4972	.4973	.4974
2.8	.4974	.4975	.4976	.4977	.4977	.4978	.4979	.4979	.4980	.4981
2.9	.4981	.4982	.4982	.4983	.4984	.4984	.4985	.4985	.4986	.4986
3.0	.4987	.4987	.4987	.4988	.4988	.4989	.4989	.4989	.4990	.4990

LAB 4
Data Transformation

◗ Tune-up

The previous labs have oriented you to the analysis of univariate distributions using SPSS. You have learned how to generate and interpret frequency distributions, statistical measures of central tendency and dispersion, as well as standard scores. All of these techniques used variables in whatever original form they were provided in the data set.

It is frequently the case, however, that you want to analyze something different from the original form of the data set. Perhaps the variable contains too many categories for your current interests. For example, perhaps the data set contains the variable 'age', but you are only interested in the three groups of ages 'young', 'middle-aged', and 'elderly'. Or perhaps you want to combine the scores of several variables together to create a new variable. This would occur, for instance, if you had several questions that inquired about 'happiness' that you wanted to combine into a 'happiness index'. Finally, perhaps you only want to analyze a selection of all the cases in a data set—for example, just women or only those who reported being 'extremely happy'.

In each of these scenarios, you will need to transform the original data so that it is more suitable for your purposes. This lab introduces you to three common data transformation procedures, including Recode, Compute, and Select, and lets you practise using each of these techniques.

LAB 4 APPLICATION

Learning Objectives

The following lab questions are directed at helping you translate the material in this lab and Section 4 of SPSS Essentials into concrete research situations. Specifically, this lab assignment challenges you to clarify your understanding of:

■ How to recode original variables into more suitable forms
■ How to compute new variables through combinations of existing variables
■ How to select a sub-sample of the cases in the data set for specific analyses

Data requirements

To conduct the analysis for this application, go to the website and download the data set 'CENSUS2001.sav'. This data set includes various kinds of information about a sample of Canadian citizens.

Introduction

Conducted every five years, the Census is important to the various levels of government because, among other things, its population estimates are used to determine the amount of transfer payments to be made from the federal government to the provinces and from the provinces to municipalities—more than $40 billion in 2001 alone.[1] The data that we are using in this application come from a random sub-sample of the Census file of individuals—our unit of analysis.[2]

A common indicator of poverty is the concept of 'crowding'. A crowded household is not only stressful to live in but is also associated with a higher rate of illness and disease. Although the incidence of crowding in Canada has decreased dramatically in the past 40 years, it remains relatively high in certain communities and population subgroups. Statistics Canada defines *crowding* (i.e., being crowded) as 'a household that contains one or more persons per room' (excluding bathrooms, hallways, and rooms used only for business purposes).[3]

In order to determine the extent of crowding, you will need to create a new variable that divides the number of people living in the dwelling by the number of rooms in the dwelling and then recode it into a second new variable with the attributes of *crowded* and *not crowded*.

Note: Before you begin, set the output display options to properly show values in your frequency distributions. (Go to *Edit* menu → *Options* → *General* → *Output Labels*. For each of the four boxes, select *Names and Labels, Values and Labels, Names and Labels, Values and Labels*, and press OK.)

Instructions

1. Run frequency distributions for the variables 'hhsize', 'rooms', and 'bnfnmemb'. Examine the distributions carefully to get a sense of what their attributes look like and the percentages of people possessing the various attributes.

2. Now let's think about the type of problem you are trying to solve. Go to the Data Editor window and look at the first case (i.e., individual) in your data set.

   a. How many people live in this person's house? _____

   b. How many rooms does the house have? _____

   c. *By hand*, calculate the number of persons per room in the house. _____

   d. According to the Statistics Canada definition, are the residents living in this household 'crowded'? Why or why not?

   _____

   _____

   _____

3. Next, let's try someone else.

   a. *By hand*, calculate the number of persons per room, for the twenty-fifth case. _____

   b. According to Statistics Canada, are they 'crowded'? Why or why not?

   _____

   _____

   _____

4. Now, let's get SPSS to give us the same information so that you don't have to do this by hand for all 79,970 cases! Using 'hhsize' and 'rooms', follow the Compute procedure outlined in SPSS Essentials to create a new (i.e., SPSS 'target') variable called 'nperoom' that calculates the number of persons per room in each respondent's household.

5. Run a frequency distribution of 'nperoom', and examine it carefully. To ensure that you understand what you just calculated:

   a. What is the lowest value in the distribution? _____
   b. If that person lived in your city, what neighbourhood do you think they might be likely to live in? Why do you say this?

   _____

   _____

   _____

   c. What is the highest value in the distribution? _____
   d. If that person lived in your city, what neighbourhood do you think they might be likely to live in? Why do you say this?

   _____

   _____

   _____

6. Using the Recode procedure, transform 'nperoom' into a new, categorical variable called 'crowding' wherein respondents are classified as living in households that are either crowded or not crowded.

7. Run a frequency distribution of 'crowding'. (Hint: Remember to compare it with 'nperoom' to ensure that you have the correct number of cases in each of your new categories.) Based on your output, answer the following question:

   What percentage of all Canadians lived in crowded households in 2001? _____%

8. Using the Select Cases procedure, select only those respondents who were members of an Indian Band or First Nation. Run a frequency distribution of 'crowding' again. Based on your output, answer the following question:

   What percentage of Indian Band/First Nations Canadians lived in crowded households in 2001? _____ %

9. Use your general sociological and/or personal knowledge to suggest reasons for the difference (if any) in the incidence of crowding between respondents who were members of a First Nations community or Indian Band and Canadians overall.

_____

_____

_____

_____

_____

_____

LAB 5
Bivariate Tables

❭ Tune-up

The previous two labs have focused on techniques related to univariate (single variable) distributions. Often, researchers want to move beyond understanding variables in isolation and are interested in the *connections between* variables. The tools and techniques for exploring the relationships between variables involve 'bivariate' (two variable) analysis.

The lab examines the most fundamental bivariate techniques—the situation when the relationship between the variables is presented in table form.

The idea of relationship

Understanding bivariate analysis begins with a clear understanding of what you intend to describe: namely, 'relationships'. This is very different from univariate analysis, which is concerned with describing the character of the separate variables.

When talking about the statistical *relationship* between variables, we are referring to the character of the *connection or structure* that links the variables. Relationships exist (in statistics as in life) when a *change in one variable is linked to a systematic change in the other variable*. Note that relationships connect two 'variables'. For a relationship to exist, it is important that within the data being examined, there is sufficient *actual variation* among the cases on both variables.

An analogy may help to solidify these points. Imagine a couple who have a relationship. You could send one of the partners to a team of clinical psychologists and have them perform a complete psychological work-up, encompassing a huge battery of psychological tests. You could then send the other partner to the same psychologists for the same testing. This would undoubtedly produce a thick file telling you a great deal about the *individual characters*—how intelligent they are, whether they are introverts or extroverts, what their anxiety levels are, and so on. In terms of the analogy, this would be the equivalent of univariate analysis, since the persons (variables) are being analyzed in isolation.

Note, however, that you could study these files endlessly but this *would not tell you about the nature of the relationship between the partners in the relationship*. Knowing how smart or stupid they are, or how introverted or extroverted they are, does not help you to find out whether they are in love or not. Love (or hate or indifference) characterizes a relationship; it tells you how a change in one person (variable) will likely produce a systematic change in the other person (variable). This is a critical point: Univariate (i.e., individual information) is qualitatively different from bivariate (i.e., relationship) information.

Elements of a relationship

When we perform an analysis on a bivariate table, we are interested in learning something about the relationship that exists between the independent and dependent variables. The relationship in a bivariate table contains two elements—*form* and *strength*. 'Form' tells you about the *structure of the relationship* between two variables; 'strength' tells you *how much difference changing one variable makes to the other variable.*

To pursue the analogy we were just using, to say that partners 'love' one another is a statement about *form*—since it characterizes the *kind of connection* they have. To say whether they are 'deeply in love' (or just moderately in love or even barely in love) is a statement about the *strength*—since it involves the intensity of the relationship. To understand a statistical relationship (or one in everyday life for that matter), you need to be able to speak to both the form and strength of the relationship.

Conventional presentation

Determining the form and strength of a relationship in a bivariate table requires that the table be presented in a 'conventional' format. By convention, bivariate tables are set up with the *independent* variable along the *top* of the table and the *dependent* variable along the *left-hand side* of the table. Using this format means that the attributes of the independent variable will be identified as the *columns* of the table, while the attributes of the dependent variable will be listed as the table's *rows*. Before you begin analyzing a bivariate table, check to ensure that the table is set up in this conventional format. Researchers, like members of almost every group, are not always 'conventional'!

Determining form

So how do you determine the form of the relationship in a bivariate table? Before beginning, you need to be sure that the conditional distributions of the independent variable are standardized. This is just a technical way of saying that the *columns within the table* must be *percentaged*. Using these percentaged columns, you proceed as follows (we can use the following table as an illustration):

Table 5.1 Community size

Marijuana legalization	Small	Large
Favourable	11%	32%
Ambivalent	29%	40%
Unfavourable	60%	28%

Look at the first (percentaged) column and imagine that it is an apartment block with as many storeys as there are rows. So in the example, you would look at the left-hand column and imagine it is an apartment block with three floors. Next, for that apartment block, let the percentages represent the number of people on each floor. In the example table, you would imagine there are 60 people on the bottom floor, 29 people on the middle floor, and 11 people on the top floor. Next, imagine that you leave the apartment block and return five minutes later. Now the distribution of the people in the apartment block is represented by the distribution of people (i.e., percentages) *in the next column*. In the example, when you return to the apartment block, there are 32 people on the top floor, 40 people on the middle floor, and 28 people on the bottom floor.

Now you ask yourself this critical question: *While you were away from the apartment, which way did the people move?* Your answer to this question comes from making an *overall assessment from comparing the two columns*. The possible answers to this question are up, down, or no change. If you apply this technique to the example, the answer is 'up'. Why? Because in the right-hand column, there are more people on the upper floors than there are in the left-hand column.

In this case, the 'up' (or in other cases, down or no change) identifies the *form* of the relationship between the variables. Now you are faced with the problem of translating what this identification of form means. To do this, you must remember that a statement about form has to state how changing the independent variable is connected to a systematic change in the dependent variable. To accomplish this, you would proceed as follows.

Draw the 'up' arrow (i.e., your conclusion from analyzing the example table) as an arrow moving at a 45-degree angle from the lower left to the upper right, with the head (tip) of the arrow at the upper right. Something like this:

Figure 5.1 'Up' arrow

Imagine that the lower end of the arrow is point A and the tip is point B. In terms of our analogy, the change (movement) of the people in the apartment block was 'up' in the sense that they walked 'up' from point A to point B.

Now, this movement from points A to B can be decomposed into a horizontal component and a vertical component. In other words, you could move from point A to B by going from point A to point C (the horizontal component) and from point C to point B (the vertical component), as illustrated in the following diagram:

Figure 5.2 Horizontal and vertical components

With this understanding, we can finally make an interpretation, using the following principles. The *horizontal* component represents the change in the *independent variable*, while the *vertical* component represents the change in the *dependent variable*. Applying this to the example table, the horizontal arrow tells us that community size (the independent variable) changes from smaller to larger (i.e., from under 100,000 to over 100,000). The vertical arrow tells us that editorial policy about legalizing marijuana (the dependent variable) changes from unfavourable toward favourable.

Putting these independent and dependent variable changes together, we derive a statement about the form of the relationship in the table. It is as follows: 'As community size increases, the editorial policy toward legalizing marijuana becomes more favourable.' This is a statement about form because it tells us how changing the independent variable is related to a systematic change in the dependent variable.

A final note about determining form in a contingency table: *You follow the same steps and logic no matter how large the table is*. If the table has more rows than the example table, you simply imagine that the apartment block has four or five floors, or whatever number. If the table has more columns than this example, then you simply repeat the 'while you were out, which way did people move?' process between every pair of adjacent columns. For example, if a table has four columns, you would compare column 1 with column 2, column 2 with column 3, and column 3 with column 4 to get the information required to determine the overall form. Remember that your final statement about form has to indicate how changing the entire independent variable is related to change in the dependent variable.

Determining strength

Once you have determined and interpreted the form of the relationship in a bivariate table (i.e., what kind of relationship it is), you can now proceed to determining the *strength* of the relationship. In the case of the example table, strength means answering the question 'How much difference does community size make to editorial policy about legalizing marijuana?' The technique for determining the strength again begins with the standardized (i.e., percentaged) bivariate table.

Your task in determining strength is to figure out how much difference there is in the dependent variable between categories of the independent variable. *To do this, you calculate the difference between the columns of the table*. For the example table, you calculate the differences between the left- and right-hand columns. Let's do this. The difference between 11 and 32 is 21, the difference between 29 and 40 is 11, and the difference between 60 and 28 is 32. Note that you perform this operation without worrying about whether the differences are positive or negative. Now we take the mean of these differences—in this case, 21 + 11 + 32 = 64, divided by 3 = 21.3 per cent. This 21.3 per cent tells you the average difference in editorial policy for communities of different sizes. This is the strength of the relationship, since it tells you how much difference community size makes to editorial policy.

After this calculation, you are left with the problem of interpretation. To interpret strength, use Table 5.2 as a guide.

Table 5.2 Guidelines for interpreting percentage differences

Amount of difference	Interpretation
Under 5%	No relationship
5–19%	Small relationship
20–34%	Modest relationship
35–55%	Moderate relationship
56–75%	Strong relationship
Over 75%	Very strong relationship

Therefore, for the example table, our 21.3 per cent difference would be interpreted the following way: 'Community size makes a modest difference to the editorial policy about legalizing marijuana.'

One final note about calculating and interpreting strength in contingency tables. If the table has more rows than the example table, this means only that you have more differences between the columns to use in computing the average difference between the columns. If the table has more columns than our example, you need to take the following steps. First, compute the average (mean) difference between columns 1 and 2. Then follow the same procedure to determine the difference between columns 2 and 3. Do this until you have the average differences between all of the adjacent columns. Finally, *take the mean (average) of these column differences to get the overall strength in the table*. Then use the little interpretive table (above) to state your conclusion about strength.

LAB 5 APPLICATION

Learning Objectives

The following lab questions are directed at helping you translate the material in this lab and Section 5 of SPSS Essentials into concrete research situations. Specifically, this lab assignment challenges you to clarify your understanding of:

- Bivariate table set-up and variation
- How to produce and interpret bivariate tables

Data requirements

To conduct the analysis for this application, go to the website and download the data set 'CENSUS2001.sav'. This data set includes various kinds of information about a sample of Canadian citizens.

Part 1: Bivariate table requirements

Table 5.3 below is an example output from a SPSS bivariate table analysis.

1. Answer the following questions:

   a. What is the independent variable in this table? _____

   b. What is the dependent variable in this table? _____

   c. What are the *attributes* of the independent variable? _____

   d. What are the *attributes* of the dependent variable? _____

   e. Interpret the number 371 in the upper right-hand cell of the table.

   f. What is the total sample size for this table? _____

   g. Is the table 'percentaged' in the correct direction? _____

      Justify your answer: _____

      _____

   h. Where in this table do you find a univariate distribution of the *dependent* variable scores?

      _____

i. How many persons of each gender are there in the sample?

Males _____ Females _____

2. How much variation (difference) is there on scores of the independent variable?

_____

3. How much variation (difference) is there on scores of the dependent variable?

_____

4. Is there sufficient variation on the variables to conduct an analysis of their relationship?

_____

Justify your answer: _____

_____

Table 5.3 'Happiness' (happiness status)* 'sex' (respondent gender) crosstabulation

			SEX		Total
			1 Male	2 Female	Total
'Happiness'	1 Happy	Count	397	371	768
		% within 'happiness'	98.0%	94.4%	96.2 %
	2 Unhappy	Count	8	22	30
		% within 'happiness'	2.0%	5.6%	3.8%
Total		Count	405	393	798
		% within 'happiness'	100.0%	100.0%	100.0%

Part 2: Examining bivariate relationships through percentage analysis

Instructions

This part has three sections. The following instructions should be applied to each section.

1. Run frequency distributions to examine each of the two variables being used. In doing so, you need to decide which variable is the independent variable and which is the dependent variable.

2. Produce a bivariate (crosstab) table that examines the effect of the independent variable on the dependent variable.

    Perform a percentage analysis of the table, using the method described in the Tune-up section. Your method needs to include an analysis of both the 'form' and the 'strength' of the relationship. Make sure to show all of your hand calculations.

3. Based on your percentage analysis, provide a brief statement that describes the relationship (if any) between your independent and dependent variables.

_____

_____

Section A: Low income cut-off status: does Indian Band/First Nations membership make *a* difference?

Statistics Canada uses a measure called the Low Income Cut-off (LICO) to allow researchers and policy-makers to measure the extent of low income in Canada. Many researchers treat the LICO as an indicator of 'poverty', although it is not a poverty line per se.

The LICO reflects a conceptual definition of poverty that means having low *household* income relative to other households of the same size, taking into consideration the amount of income a Canadian family needs in order to provide basic necessities (food, clothing, shelter).[1] Some commentators argue that the LICO generates rates of poverty that are inordinately high because of the way that it is calculated, while others defend the measure as the best one that we currently have.

Suppose that we are interested in whether low-income status (i.e., the respondent's household income either falls beneath the Low Income Cut-off or it does not) differs between individuals who are members of an Indian Band/First Nation and those who are not. Use the variables 'bnfnmemb' and 'licostat' to examine this possibility.

Hand calculations of output to determine form and strength
Statement of Conclusion:

_____

_____

_____

Section B: Does the amount of time spent on housework differ between men and women?

Sociologists of the family have often noted that aside from arguments over money, household chores are one of the most frequent sources of conflict within couples. Use the variables 'sex' and 'unpaid' to see what Canadians who were married or cohabiting had to say about this issue. (Note: You will see a lot of 'not applicable' cases because respondents who were not married or cohabiting are not included in our analysis, nor were some respondents, such as those under age 18, asked about housework. Do not worry about those cases, since they will be automatically excluded from all of your analyses in this section.)

Hand calculations of output to determine form and strength
Statement of Conclusion:

_____

_____

_____

Section C: Does obtaining a university degree pay off?

One of the reasons, although certainly not the only reason, that people attend university is the hope that it will lead to an occupation that provides them with a good income. We can investigate this connection today because Statistics Canada asked Census respondents to indicate the highest level of schooling that they have completed (there were 14 possible levels, ranging from no schooling to a postgraduate degree). In the data set, these different education levels have been grouped into three categories as the ordinal variable 'educats'.

Statistics Canada also asked respondents to disclose their most recent annual personal income before taxes. In the data set, this original ratio-level variable, which was measured to the exact dollar, has been transformed into a three-category ordinal variable called 'incats'. Please note that you will find many 'not applicable' cases because minors, for example, were not asked these questions. You can safely ignore these cases.

Hand calculations of output to determine form and strength
Statement of Conclusion:

_____

_____

_____

Part 3: Preparing variables for crosstabulation

Suppose that you are working for a marketing firm and are interested in finding out which people are more (or less) 'well-off' financially. You are particularly interested in the differences among younger, middle-aged, and older people. Knowing a respondent's specific age is less important to you than knowing their stage in the life course, since different stages are connected with different occupational paths (early career with little seniority versus late career with seniority but working fewer hours or already retired and living on a pension, for example).

For this reason alone, you want to group the age data. You decide to group respondents into three categories that reflect different life stages:

18–39; 40–59; 60+

But you need to group the data for other reasons as well. To see why, take the variable 'age' and run a bivariate crosstabulation with the variable 'incats'. With the output crosstabulation, make an interpretation of the results.

Form:

_____

_____

Strength:

_____

_____

In all likelihood, you had serious problems performing an interpretation of your results. What problems did you have?

_____

_____

The problems you encountered are common mistakes that students learning about data analysis make. To appreciate how to overcome the problems and generate more meaningful results, the following section asks you to group 'age' to make it more suitable for bivariate crosstabulation. Before doing so, use the Select Cases procedure to limit your sample to adults (age 18+).

Instructions

1. Using the SPSS Recode procedure, transform 'age' into a new variable (let's call it 'agegrp') that is grouped into the three categories described earlier. As usual, ensure that your new variable has proper labels, etc.

2. Record your frequency results for 'agegrp' below:

   18–39: _____ (n); _____(%)

   40–59: _____ (n); _____(%)

   60+:   _____ (n); _____(%)

3. Produce a contingency table that examines the effect of age ('agegrp') on income ('incats').

4. Look at your table, and draw a conclusion about the generally 'best' time of the life course, or the 'prime of life', financially speaking. (You do not need to do a percentage analysis; simply looking at the patterns in the table will suffice here.)

   Conclusion:

   _____

   _____

   _____

Part 4: Comparing means

In the previous section, we examined the relationship between education and income when both were presented as categorical variables. What if you had a more precise measure of income? In this data set, we have access to income at the interval/ratio level (i.e., before it was collapsed into categories) and also educational level at the ordinal level. In order to compare income by educational level, we need to use a different procedure, one that is not described in SPSS Essentials. This procedure is known as the 'Means' procedure.

Note: Readers should bear in mind that in this sample, 'income' is positively skewed, which can pose problems when using Means. However, an examination of the data did not reveal substantial outliers. Most samples show a positive skew to income, where there tends to be a relatively higher number of individuals with relatively high rather than relatively low income, and this is not necessarily due to very extreme or atypical values.

Instructions

1. In SPSS, go to the *Analyze* tab and scroll down to select Compare Means → Means. This procedure allows you to compare the means of a quantitative (normally interval/ratio) variable with that of a qualitative (normally nominal/ordinal) variable.

2. Place the variable 'income' (total personal income before taxes) into the Dependent List box.

3. Place the variable 'educats' (education level, grouped) into the Independent List box.

4. Select the *Options* tab, and select the ANOVA Table and ETA box; click OK.

5. In your output, you will see a table called 'Report'. Using that table, calculate the difference between mean incomes for:

   a. Individuals with a maximum of a high school diploma and those with at least some post-secondary education but no degree: $_____

   b. Individuals with some post-secondary education but no degree and those with a university degree: $_____

   c. Individuals with a maximum of a high school diploma and those with a university degree: $_____

6. What do these data say about the relationship between education and income?

   _____

   _____

   _____

   _____

LAB 6
Trivariate Tables

▶ Tune-up

The descriptive analytical techniques you have learned so far include single variable (univariate) and single relationship, two-variable (bivariate) procedures. These techniques have been useful in describing the nature of the evidence (data) collected. So far, so good. But more sophisticated research questions require more sophisticated analytical techniques, which is what trivariate analysis provides.

The goal of science

Trivariate techniques are the basic form of 'multivariate' analysis. Multivariate analysis includes three or more variables simultaneously. Once you master the trivariate case, all multivariate techniques simply extend the logic to take additional variables into account.

To understand the place and importance of trivariate analysis, you need to remind yourself what the goal of science—a method of knowing—is. Science is only one method of knowing; it is not the only method. The credibility of science as a way of knowing rests on its purported superior ability to describe and explain things the way they 'really' are. This claim is what has brought science to the prestigious position it has held in recent centuries. In medicine, engineering, physics, psychology, biology, sociology, and so on, the extensive gains in the knowledge base over time are attributable to the application of the scientific method.

It should be evident, then, that any academic discipline that calls itself a 'science' (i.e., any of the natural or social sciences) is very concerned with protecting its ability to distinguish claims that are 'false' from those that are 'true'. Most important, for a science, is to avoid declaring that something is 'true' when in fact it is 'false'. Such errors can dramatically detract from the credibility of science. For instance, if a scientific study declares that a particular drug cures cancer when in fact it does not, the credibility of science is affected. The same applies when science incorrectly claims that a particular reading method is superior to another or a particular study method is superior. If such claims are later found wanting, the value of the stock of science declines.

This emphasis on getting things 'correct' is really a way of saying that science is concerned with making 'authentic' statements. 'Authenticity' occurs when the way things 'appear' is the way things actually 'are'. Here, authenticity in science is the same as it is with people—appearances match reality. Phoney, inauthentic people are those who appear one way (e.g., pretend they are your friends) when in fact they are not. In the same way, inauthentic statements in science appear as one type when in fact they are another.

As anyone who has ever been 'fooled' or 'conned' by others can attest, it is not easy to distinguish authentic people from inauthentic ones. It often takes time and further information to discern who is genuine and who is not. The same is true in science. Once you have identified a particular type of bivariate relationship, it takes further research (which, incidentally, literally means 'to look again') to determine whether what 'appears' to be a particular kind of relationship between two variables is 'actually' that kind of relationship. The techniques of the 'elaboration model' that include trivariate analysis help to assess the authenticity of bivariate relationships.

The general logic of multivariate analysis

Multivariate analysis occurs after bivariate analysis. The goal of multivariate analysis is to determine whether or not the bivariate relationship you have identified is authentic or something else. In other words, *the purpose of multivariate analysis is to determine what, if any, effect 'other' variables are having on the independent–dependent variable relationship*.

To be clear about what is meant by 'other variables', let's look at the following table, which displays the relationship between individuals' social status and whether they vote for conservative or liberal parties. This is a simple bivariate table that you could analyze with the techniques you have already learned.

Table 6.1 Social status and voting pattern

Voting	Social status		
	Low	High	Total
conservative	150	242	392
liberal	111	78	189
Total	261	320	581

For now, however, look at the number 150 in the upper-left cell of the table. What does this number mean?

It means that in this study of 581 individuals, 150 persons with low social status voted for a conservative party. Now imagine that these 150 individuals were actually in a room somewhere and you could see them. Do you think they would be of the same gender or of different genders? The same height or different heights? The same level of education or different levels?

The answer is that they would probably be different with respect to gender, height, education, and all manner of other variables.

Now imagine having the 242 people in the upper-right cell in a similar room. Are they likely to be of different genders, heights, education levels, etc.? How about the 111 individuals in the lower-left cell and the 78 people in the lower-right category?

The answer, in all cases, is that the members of each of the cells in the table will contain different genders, heights, and education levels. This is an important appreciation, because what it tells you is that gender, education, and height (to choose just a few properties) *are variables within this table*. This is important, because since they are variables, they can change *and by changing (i.e., varying) they might be affecting the relationship observed between social class (the independent variable) and voting pattern (the dependent variable).*

This is a crucial point. *Wherever variables are operating (i.e., changing), they might be having an effect on an apparent relationship.* This idea holds as true in human relationships as it does in statistical ones. For instance, if one partner tells the other they 'love' him (or her), she or he is making a statement about the kind of relationship they have. But this may or may not be an authentic statement. If the receiver of the declaration doesn't trust the sender or is suspicious or naive, that person might imagine that someone else (who is a 'variable' in the sense that he or she is living) had told the sender to tell the receiver to make a declaration of love merely to mask the fact that they are having an affair.

In general, *it is always possible that any apparent relationship may be affected by the operation of other variables.* In the case of the relationship between social status and voting patterns in the previous table, perhaps education or gender is affecting the relationship. In the case of the 'loving' partners, perhaps some Person X is affecting the relationship.

The question becomes: How can we be sure whether an observed relationship is authentic or not? The logic of multivariate analysis is intended to answer this question.

The general logic of multivariate analysis is straightforward. It requires you to compare the relationship between the independent and dependent variable under two sets of conditions—first, when some 'other' (third) variable is allowed to vary (change) and second, when this third variable is held constant (not allowed to vary/change).

The first condition is satisfied in what is called the *original relationship*, where original relationship means the bivariate relationship. This is the condition we observed in the first table. In this bivariate table, we can examine the relationship between the independent variable (social status) and the dependent variable (voting pattern) but under the condition where a third variable (gender, for instance) is varying.

The second condition requires that we look at the same relationship (i.e., between the same independent and dependent variables) but where the 'other' variable (i.e., the one we suspect might be affecting the original relationship) is held constant. This condition is met with the creation of *partial relationships*. The tables below illustrate partial relationships.

Table 6.2 Social status and voting pattern *for males*

Voting	Social status		
	Low	**High**	**Total**
conservative	37	14	51
liberal	56	14	70
Total	93	28	121

Table 6.3 Social status and voting pattern *for females*

Voting	Social status		
	Low	**High**	**Total**
conservative	113	228	341
liberal	55	64	119
Total	168	292	460

There are several things to be noted about partial relationships—in this case partial *tables*, since the data are at lower levels of measurement. First, note that they are called 'partial' because they are 'parts' of the whole (i.e., the original relationship). You can see this by noting that if you add up the frequencies in any particular cells of the partial tables, you obtain the frequency in that cell in the original relationship. For instance, the lower right cell partial table cells (14 + 64) equal the total (78) for that cell in the original table. The same is true for all equivalent cells in the tables.

Second, note that in each partial table, the third ('other') variable is *held constant* (in this example, gender is held constant). (Incidentally, sometimes this 'other' variable is called a 'test' variable, since it indicates the condition under which you are 'testing' the validity of the original relationship.) To demonstrate this to yourself, imagine the 37 individuals of low social status who voted conservative in the 'males' table. If you gathered these folks together, you would see that they are all males. The same is true for all the other cells in that table. In other words, in the 'males' table, we can observe the relationship between social status and voting pattern under the condition where gender has no effect. The same is true in the 'females' table, since all those included in this partial table are females.

In summary, this is the way multivariate relationship analysis is set up. There is always some original (bivariate) relationship. And there is a set of partial relationships in which the relationship between the independent and dependent variables can be observed without the potentially contaminating effects of some third variable. Incidentally, in a multivariate analysis, *there will always be as many partial relationships as there are attributes (values) of the third variable*. The reason that there were two partial tables in our example is that 'gender' has two attributes (male and female). If we controlled for some other variable (for example, education, which might have three values, 'low', 'medium', and 'high'), there would then be three partial relationships.

A few other points before we turn our attention to analysis. First, the logic of multivariate analysis uses what is called the 'elaboration model or paradigm'. This logic of 'elaboration' gets its name from taking other (test) variables into account to see what (if any) impact they have on the original (bivariate) relationship. Second, the same idea of elaboration holds no matter what the level of measurement of the variables. Our example used original and partial *tables*, since the variables were at lower levels of measurement. If the variables were at higher levels of measurement, we would create, for example, original and partial *correlations* rather than tables.

Multivariate analysis

With the original and partial relationships in place, you are now in a position to perform a multivariate analysis, which involves analyzing the relationships to determine what effect (if any) the test variable has on the original relationship. This analysis is performed through the following steps:

1. Analyze and interpret each of the original and partial relationships *separately*.
2. Based on the results of your analysis in step 1, *compare the partial relationships to each other*.
3. Based on the results of your analysis in step 1, *compare the partial relationships to the original relationship*.
4. Based on your comparisons in steps 2 and 3, *select a model that best fits the effects occurring among the independent, dependent, and test variables*.

What does each of these steps entail? Step 1 is easy, since you already have the tools at your disposal. The original relationship is simply a bivariate relationship, and you have already learned how to analyze this type of connection between an independent and dependent variable. The partial relationships are analyzed using the same tools, since they involve identifying the nature of the connection between the same independent and dependent variable as in the original relationship. Steps 2 and 3 involve taking your interpretations of the separate original and partial relationship analyses (step 1) and comparing the results. The basic idea is to determine whether the partial relationships are similar to, or different from, each other (step 2) and to determine whether the partial relationships are similar to, or different from, the original relationship (step 3). With these comparisons in place, you select a model (step 4) that most closely fits the results of the comparisons you made in steps 2 and 3.

To execute step 4, however, requires an appreciation of various possibilities you might encounter, which is the next topic.

Accounting schemes

Remember that the goal of the comparison analysis you are performing in multivariate analysis is to see what effect (if any) the test variable has on the original independent–dependent variable relationship. This is really what you are trying to see in steps 2 and 3, since what you are doing is comparing the independent–dependent variable relationship under the conditions where the test variable changes (i.e., the original relationship) and where it is held constant (i.e., the partial relationships). When you make these comparisons, the potential types of effects you might observe are limitless. In other words, it is theoretically possible for a third variable to have an enormous range of possible effects on the original relationship. To draw an analogy with everyday life, the potential effects that a third person can have on your relationship with your sweetheart are similarly wide.

Fortunately, however, in research as in everyday life, *the actual effects of third variables tend to fall into a fairly limited number of possibilities*. These possibilities are called 'accounting schemes', since they are the models that help 'account for' the effect that the test variable may be having on the original relationship. To select the appropriate accounting scheme (step 4) for a particular set of data requires that you understand (1) what the possible accounting schemes are, and (2) how they reveal themselves in the steps 2 and 3 comparisons. We will now discuss these two features for each of a standard set of accounting schemes.

Authentic relationships

One possible relationship between the independent and dependent variable is that the relationship is 'authentic'. Authentic relationships in statistical analysis, as in everyday life, are those that are 'genuine', which means that the way they appear is the way they actually are. This feature of authentic relationships means that when tested, they are 'unaffected' (i.e., they remain the same). In everyday circumstances, this is the sign of authentic relationships between people. If someone is genuinely your friend, they remain your friend under all kinds of conditions (i.e., 'tests'), including whether you are sick or healthy or whether you are rich or poor, etc.

When making the comparisons among the original and partial relationships (steps 2 and 3), the sign of an authentic relationship is 'replication'. That is, whatever connection you observe between the independent and dependent variables in the original relationship, you find the same or similar connection in the partial relationships.

Spurious relationships

Not all relationships are authentic, however; some relationships are not what they initially appear to be. One possibility is that an original relationship is fake or phoney, which is what the term 'spurious' means. Spurious relationships occur when a third variable causes changes in the independent variable and causes changes in the dependent variable. In the spurious case, the nature of the relationship observed between the independent and dependent variables is different, depending on whether the test variable is allowed to vary (as in the original relationship) or is held constant (as in the partial relationships). Since in the spurious case, the third variable is causing changes in both the independent and dependent variables, a connection will appear in the original relationship (i.e., a change in the independent variable will be associated with a systematic change in the dependent variable). However, when the test variable is held constant (i.e., in the partial relationships), the independent–dependent variable will largely or completely disappear. This disappearance will occur because the source of the apparent connection between the independent and dependent variables (i.e., the test variable) is no longer allowed to have its influence (i.e., it is controlled).

When making the comparisons among the original and partial relationships (steps 2 and 3), the sign of a spurious relationship is as follows: whatever connection you observe between the independent and dependent variables in the original relationship disappears or largely disappears in the partial relationships. To be more specific, when you compare the partial relationships to one another (step 2), they are the same as one another and show little or no relationship. When you compare the partials to the original relationship (step 3), these relationships are different from one another—there is some relationship in the original and little or no relationship in the partials.

Sometimes spurious relationships are called 'explanation'. This is an appropriate synonym, because the test variable 'explains' why there is an apparent original relationship between the independent and dependent variables when, in fact, no such connection exists.

Intervening relationships

The 'intervening' model of the relationships among the independent, dependent, and control variables is also known by the synonym 'interpretation'. If you and I do not share a common language, we require an 'interpreter' to 'intervene'. Your message would have to be translated through the interpreter to reach me in a meaningful way. In a parallel fashion, in the intervening model the independent variable affects the test variable, which in turn influences the dependent variable.

With this model in mind, it should be clear that if the effects of the intervening (test) variable are removed, then the relationship between the independent and dependent variables disappears. However, if the intervening variable is allowed to do its work, then a meaningful connection between the independent and dependent variables is established.

It turns out that the empirical pattern among the original and partial relationships for the 'intervening/interpretation' model is the same as it is for the 'spurious/explanation' model. This pattern is as follows: an apparent relationship is observed in the original connection between the independent and dependent variables, but this connection is reduced to zero or near zero in the partial relationships. In other words, the test variable is making all the difference in whether or not there is an observable connection between the independent and dependent variables, just as an interpreter makes all the difference in whether two people who don't share a common language can communicate.

The fact that the empirical patterns for the spurious/explanation and intervening/interpretation relationships are the same means that *you cannot tell which is operating simply by looking at the empirical evidence*. If this empirical pattern is evident, you know that the accounting scheme is one or the other, but you don't know which one it is. But you still have to make a decision, and the way you do this is by taking an additional consideration into account.

The distinguishing feature between the spurious/explanation model and the intervening/interpretation model is *the time-ordering (sequence) of the variables*. In the *spurious* model, the *test variable changes first*, followed by a change in the independent and dependent variables. In the *intervening* model, the *independent variable changes first*, followed by changes in the test variable and then the dependent variable. The empirical evidence does not tell you which time-ordering is occurring; *to make this determination, you have to use either theory or common sense*. If your research is guided by a theory, the theory will often suggest the anticipated sequential ordering of the variables. If you don't have such a theory, you need to stop and think. For example, if the independent variable is 'early childhood experience' and the test variable is 'level of education', it is pretty clear what the sequencing of these variables must be.

Interaction relationships

The three accounting schemes discussed so far share a common feature that may not be immediately evident. In all cases *when the partial relationships are compared to one another (step 2), they are similar*. In the case of the authentic model, they are similar in that they display some relationship between the independent and dependent variables. In the cases of the spurious and intervening models, they are similar in that they display little or no relationship between the independent and dependent variables.

The 'interaction' accounting scheme (also called 'specification') is different in that for this model, *the partial relationships are different from one another*. The feature means that *the connection between the independent and dependent variables changes, depending on which value of the test variable is under consideration*.

In terms of the decision model presented earlier, the outcomes evident when the interaction/specification model is operational include the following:

Step 2: The partial relationships will be different from one another. Typically, one or more partials will display a relationship, while the other partial(s) will be at or near no relationship.

Step 3: The partial relationships will be different from the original. Typically, one or more partials will display the same or a stronger relationship than the original, while the other partial(s) will display much less or no relationship.

Other Possibilities

These four accounting schemes are the ones typically evident in data. Other possibilities may be included in your standard text, including 'distorter' and 'suppressor' models. However, these alternatives are not very commonly seen in actual empirical evidence.

Selecting a Model

The final step in our multivariate analysis decision model (step 4) requires that you select a model from among the accounting schemes that best fits the empirical patterns evident in the data. The emphasis here is on the 'best fits' idea.

The accounting scheme models described here and in your textbook are 'ideal' cases in the sense that they capture what a 'perfect' authentic or spurious or intervening or other model is like. Real empirical data (like real human relationships) are typically imperfect. This imperfection, however, does not absolve us from having to make decisions regarding what is occurring.

We still claim, for example, that we are in 'love' with someone, even when our love may be imperfect.

The same idea applies to selecting an operational model in multivariate analysis. You need to select a model that is *most closely approximated* by the empirical evidence.

In conclusion, remember to proceed in the following way:

1. *Analyze the data* using the multivariate techniques described.
2. *Select an accounting scheme model* that is most closely approximated by your data. *Justify your choice* of a multivariate model.
3. *Explain what the model* you have selected means in terms of the variables involved.

LAB 6 APPLICATION

Learning Objectives

The following lab questions are directed at helping you translate the material in this lab and Section 6 of SPSS Essentials into concrete research situations. Specifically, this lab assignment challenges you to clarify your understanding of:

- Generating bivariate and trivariate tables
- Using the logic of multivariate analysis to determine the effects of third variables

Data requirements

To conduct the analysis for this application, go to the website and download the data set 'GSS2001.sav'. This data set includes various kinds of information about a sample of Canadian citizens.

Introduction

This exercise utilizes a sub-sample of data from the 2001 *General Social Survey (Cycle 15)*, conducted by Statistics Canada. Respondents who at the time of the survey had never been married or who were previously married, were not currently in an intimate relationship, and had never lived common-law were asked the following question:

Do you think you could ever live in a common-law relationship?

The results showed that 47.9 per cent of respondents said 'Yes' while 52.1 per cent said 'No'. These figures suggest an interesting dependent variable to explore further, because not only is it an interesting topic but the data also have good *variability*. After all, the objective of bivariate and multivariate analyses is to find out why individuals think, feel, or act differently or know *different* things from other people. Respondents were asked a number of questions that might provide clues, including their sex, age, and other socio-demographic variables. The following application will conduct a trivariate analysis of these data.

Instructions

1. Run frequency distributions of 'sex' (sex of respondent) and 'willing' (willingness to live common-law), and examine them carefully. (Do not worry if you have a lot of 'not applicables'; remember that not everyone in the sample was asked this question.)

2. Perform a bivariate crosstabulation that examines the effect of 'sex' on 'willing', and record your percentage results in the table below.

Table 6.4 Willingness to live common-law, by sex of respondent

Willingness to live common-law	Sex of respondent	
	Male	Female
Yes		
No		
Total		

3. Summarize the original, bivariate (zero-order) relationship by filling in the blanks below. Use the 'Guidelines for Interpreting Percentage Differences' (Table 5.2) in Lab 5.

   Percentage difference between sexes: _____

   Form of the relationship: _____

   Interpretation of the relationship:

   _____

   _____

4. Think of a possible sociological explanation for your results. Why did you get them? What do you think they say about society?

   _____

   _____

   _____

   _____

   _____

5. What if we control for religiosity, conceptualized as religious service attendance? The variable 'rlattend' (religious attendance) categorizes respondents as attending religious services 'at least once a week' or 'less than once a week' (including never attending). Next, run a trivariate

crosstabulation between 'sex' and 'willing', controlling for 'rlattend'.[1] Transcribe your percentage results below. (Note: The following table is formatted in a way that is similar to most textbook examples and is easier to interpret than the SPSS output.)

Table 6.5 Willingness to live common-law, by respondent's sex and religious attendance

Willingness to live common-law	Once a week		Less than once a week	
	Male	Female	Male	Female
Yes				
No				
Total				

6. Summarize the partial relationships by filling in the blanks below.

   Percentage difference between sexes: _____

   Form of the relationship: _____

   Interpretation of the relationship:

   _____

   _____

7. Compare the results in the partials with the original, bivariate results, and circle the best answer, noted in capital letters below:

(1) SAME

(partial relationships are essentially the same strength as the original relationship)

(2) LESS OR NONE

(partial relationships are zero or substantially weaker than those found in the original relationship)

(3) SPLIT

(one of the partials is the same or stronger than the original relationship, and the other is weaker or zero)

8. Name the accounting scheme (model) that best summarizes your findings. Justify your choice.

   Model: _____

   Justification of choice:

   _____

   _____

   _____

9. Pretend that the person reading this application has a basic working knowledge of statistics and its terminology but has no knowledge of the logic of multivariate analysis. Set aside the name of the model that you chose; it will not mean anything to them. Instead, *describe* your model as clearly and as succinctly as you can (two or three sentences) with reference to your specific findings.

   _____

   _____

   _____

   _____

   As well, thinking sociologically, *explain* why you think you got those results (in one or two sentences). (Hint: The reason behind this task is to help you understand the crucial role of *statistical control* in establishing causal relationships, not merely to crunch numbers without being able to fully comprehend and interpret patterns among them.)

   _____

   _____

   _____

   _____

   _____

LAB 7
PRE Measures for Crosstabs

▶ Tune-up

Why PRE measures

Lab 5 focused on the basic tools for examining the relationship between two variables when they are in table (crosstabular) form. These basic tools use percentage analysis. As useful as these techniques are, they are not as sophisticated as we might like. In the case of contingency tables, imagining people's movement between floors of a building (to determine form) is rather crude, and the percentage difference technique (to determine strength) is rather imprecise.

Providing more efficient and effective solutions to the interpretation of bivariate relationships rests on the use of PRE measures of association. PRE stands for 'proportional reduction of error' and represents a 'family' of different statistics that inform you about bivariate relationships.

The PRE family

A first point to appreciate about PRE statistics is that they are a 'family'. This means that although the specific statistics in this family are distinct, they share a set of common characteristics. To understand these shared characteristics, we need some fundamental ideas about variables, relationships, and predictions.

You will recall that bivariate relationships tell us about the connection between two variables. The dependent variable in the relationship is the variable whose values (attributes, scores) we are interested in predicting. Since the dependent variable is a 'variable', its scores vary across different cases. For instance, if the dependent variable is 'research methods grades', then we expect (because it is a variable) that different students will receive different grades. Now our question becomes: How do we predict a particular person's grades in research methods? (In general, how do we predict an individual's score on the dependent variable?)

One way that we can make such a prediction is from general information about the distribution of scores on the dependent variable. If examined by itself, the dependent variable is a single variable, which means that it can be thought of as a univariate distribution. So one answer to our prediction question 'how do we predict an individual's score on the dependent variable (research methods grades)?' is to do so from information about the dependent variable distribution. For instance, we might use a prediction rule like 'predict the average (i.e., mean) score on the dependent variable' as our rule, in which case we would predict (guess) that your score in research methods would be the mean (average) score. This is a reasonable prediction, since if we don't have any other information it is reasonable to predict that any person is probably 'average'. If you don't know anything about a person and are asked to predict their height or weight, isn't it reasonable to predict that he or she is probably of average height or weight?

When you make predictions about dependent variable scores this way (i.e., using only information about the dependent variable distribution), you are using what is called a *marginal prediction rule*. This is, however, not the only way in which you might make a prediction about a dependent variable score (in our example, a research methods grade). If the dependent variable is related to an independent variable, then if you knew a person's independent variable score, you might be able to make a prediction about a person's dependent variable score. For instance, if I know that studying (an independent variable) has a direct relationship to grades (the dependent variable) and if I know that you studied a lot, I might then predict that you will do better than average in research methods. Using information about how the independent variable is related to the dependent variable to make predictions about the dependent variable is called a *relational prediction rule*.

These are the first two shared characteristics that all statistics in the PRE 'family' have. Each of them has a marginal prediction rule, and each has a relational prediction rule. In other words, each has some way of predicting the dependent variable from its own distribution, and each has a way of predicting the dependent variable from information about the independent variable.

Now, remember that marginal and relational prediction rules are just means of making predictions about scores on the dependent variable. If we used the marginal prediction rule 'predict average grade' on all students in research methods, we would make many errors, since many students' grades are not 'average' (that is, on the mean). Likewise, if we used the relational prediction rule 'more studying means higher grades', we would make errors in predicting students' grades as well. In fact, not all students who study a lot do well, and not all students who study a little do poorly. These points illustrate the third feature of all PRE measures of association: *they have a way of counting prediction errors*. Specifically, they have a way of counting two kinds of errors: *marginal prediction rule errors (designated as E1) and relational prediction rule errors (designated as E2)*.

The fourth and final feature shared by all PRE measures of association is that *their statistical result can be calculated or interpreted using the following general formula*:

$$PRE = \frac{E_1 - E_2}{E_1}$$

Let us look at this formula for a minute and see what it says. First you determine how many errors you make using the marginal prediction rule (E1). This tells you how many errors you make predicting people's scores on the dependent variable *when you do not have any information about the independent variable*. Then you determine how many errors you make using the relational prediction rule (E2). This tells you how many errors you make predicting dependent variable scores *when you know the independent variable and its relationship to the dependent variable*. The *difference* between these errors (i.e., E1 − E2) tells you *how many fewer errors (mistakes) you make predicting the dependent variable when you know the independent variable, as opposed to when you do not know the independent variable.*

To go back to our example, if we make 30 errors predicting students' research methods grades by guessing that each student's score is the mean (i.e., using the marginal prediction rule) and we make 15 errors by predicting each student's score on the basis of how much he or she studied (i.e., using the relational prediction rule), we have then reduced our errors by 15 (E1 − E2 = 30 − 15). Now, let us be very clear what this means: This 'improvement' in prediction (i.e., reduction in errors) occurs *because of the relationship of the independent variable to the dependent variable.* In other words, if the independent variable were unrelated to the dependent variable (for instance, if instead of asking you how much you studied, I gathered information about how much you liked ice cream), there would then be no reduction in errors between E1 and E2. This is a critical point: *The stronger the relationship the independent variable has to the dependent variable, the greater will be the reduction in prediction errors.* If, for instance, studying was perfectly related to grades, then knowing how much you studied would allow us to completely eliminate all prediction errors.

Next, notice that the PRE formula divides E1 − E2 by E1. The numerator of the equation provides you with the actual reduction in errors. The magnitude of this result, however, is entirely a function of how many cases for which you are making predictions. If your study contained 50 subjects, you would almost certainly get a smaller result than if your study contained 500 subjects. The PRE makes a correction to adjust for this fact. Instead of being a 'reduction in error' statistic, it is a '*proportional* reduction in error' statistic. Proportions help to make results comparable and, when multiplied by 100, become percentages. So by using the PRE formula, we can determine what percentage of errors are being reduced thanks to our use of how the independent and dependent variables are related. And as we said previously, this information provides insights into the character of the relationship between the variables.

To summarize, all statistics included in the PRE family of statistics have the following four common features:

- a marginal prediction rule;
- a relational prediction rule;
- a way of counting errors for both marginal and relational prediction rules; and
- the use of a common formula: PRE = (E1 − E2) / E1.

These four features are shared by all PRE measures of association. There are differences, however, in the application and calculation of different specific statistics in this family of measures. The *differences* in these statistics are derived from the fact that the *specific* marginal and prediction rules are different for each statistic and the *specific* ways of counting errors are different. In short, the specific members of this family of statistics are unique, but they all share a common template.

Selecting PRE measures

Different PRE statistics are applicable to variables measured at different levels of measurement. Therefore, the appropriate selection and application of PRE measures requires that you be able to identify the level of measurement of both the independent and the dependent variable.

There are a large number of statistics in the PRE family, since there are a large number of possible combinations of independent and dependent variable types. This lab addresses two measures in the PRE family that are appropriate (1) where both independent and dependent variables are nominal and (2) where both variables are ordinal.

Understanding lambda

Lambda is an appropriate PRE statistic to use when both the independent and the dependent variable are measured at the nominal level. This is not the place to demonstrate how lambda is calculated. Instead, we will concentrate on understanding its application and interpretation.

Since lambda is a PRE measure of association, it must have a marginal prediction rule, a relational prediction rule, and ways of counting the errors made using each rule. The calculation of lambda uses the following understanding:

Marginal prediction rule: Lambda uses the following marginal prediction rule: *Predict the modal category of the dependent variable.* From your understanding of univariate statistics, you will recall that the mode of a distribution is the category of the variable that occurs most frequently. To apply the marginal prediction rule, the other point you need to know is that given the way bivariate tables are conventionally presented, the univariate distribution of the dependent variable is found on the outside, right margin of the table (i.e., the column of numbers on the right, outside section of the table).

So to apply the marginal prediction rule (i.e., to predict the value of all cases on the dependent variable when you only know the distribution of scores on the dependent variable [i.e., its frequency distribution]), you choose the category with the highest frequency on the dependent variable.

Relational prediction rule: Lambda uses the following relational prediction rule: *Predict the modal category of each conditional distribution of the independent variable.* To understand this rule, you need to know the meaning of a 'conditional distribution of the independent variable'. If you look at any bivariate table, you will notice that the columns of the table are distributions of the dependent variable *for specific values of the independent variable.* The columns inside the table are conditional distributions of the independent variable; in other words, they tell you how the dependent variable is distributed under a *specific condition* of the independent variable.

With this in mind, we can now interpret what lambda's relational prediction rule means. It means choosing the most frequently occurring category of the dependent variable for each specific value of the independent variable.

Ways of counting errors (E1 and E2): For lambda, the number of errors made using the marginal prediction rule (E1) is *all the cases that do not fall into the modal category of the dependent variable distribution.* The number of errors using the relational prediction rule (E2) is *all cases that do not fall into the modal category of all the conditional distributions of the independent variable.*

Now that you have E1 and E2, to calculate lambda you simply apply the general PRE formula = (E1 − E2) / E1.

Interpreting lambda

You now know how PRE calculates the PRE statistic called lambda. This is significant, but it is incomplete. To complete your understanding, you need to be able to interpret the meaning of the statistic.

Lambda has a conventional interpretation in which 'conventional' means the opposite of 'idiosyncratic'. The 'conventionality' of lambda's interpretation occurs because it is a member of the PRE family of statistics, and all members of this family share a common interpretive framework.

The interpretation of all PRE-based statistics begins the same way, with the phrase 'You proportionately reduce your errors by _____ per cent . . .' The _____ (blank) in this sentence is the actual value of the statistic that you have calculated, multiplied by 100. For example, if the calculated lambda value were 0.67, the interpretation would begin 'You proportionately reduce your errors by 67 per cent . . .'.

To complete the remainder of the interpretation statement, we need to think about what was completed in the calculation. Recall that what the calculation of lambda did was make a comparison. It compared how well the dependent variable could be predicted under two conditions: first, without knowledge of the independent variable and second, with knowledge of the independent variable. This comparison process needs to be expressed in the interpretation of lambda.

So let us apply this understanding to a lambda of 0.67 expressing the relationship between gender and employment status. Such an interpretation would read 'You proportionately reduce your errors by 67 per cent when you know people's gender as opposed to not knowing their gender when predicting employment status.'

One final point about interpreting lambda. Under the discussion of bivariate tables, we noted that interpreting the relationship between two variables at the lower (nominal or ordinal) levels of measurement had to speak to two issues: strength and form. The PRE interpretation of lambda only speaks to the concept of strength. This leaves the question: How do you find the form of the relationship in a table where lambda is the appropriate PRE measure of association?

It is worth noting that in *some* PRE measures of association, information about form is built into the output of the statistical calculation. Unfortunately, this is not the case for lambda. Consequently, for tables that you calculate lambda, you must identify and interpret the form of the relationship using the 'apartment' technique discussed in Lab 5.

A caution about using lambda

All statistical techniques have strengths and weaknesses. One potential problem with lambda is that it can result in 'false zeros'. A false zero occurs when you calculate the lambda statistic and get a PRE result of zero, even though a relationship actually exists between the variables. Under this circumstance, the zero result is 'false', because it indicates that no relationship exists between the variables when there actually is a relationship.

Such false zeros are calculation oddities, and we need not concern ourselves here with why they occasionally occur. What is important for you to appreciate are the following points:

- false zeros can occur when calculating lambda.
- Not all lambda values of zero are false (i.e., lambda can also produce 'true [correct] zeros').

Given that lambda can produce both true and false zeros, you are faced with the issue of how you should proceed if the lambda you calculate is zero. In this circumstance, proceed as follows:

- When you get a lambda result of zero, recalculate the relationship between the variables using the 'percentage down, compare across' technique introduced in Lab 5.
- If the percentaging technique gives you a result of zero (or near zero), conclude that the lambda result is a true zero.
- If the percentaging technique gives you a result that shows a substantial (i.e., non-zero) relationship, conclude that the lambda is a false zero.
- If you conclude that the lambda is a false zero, then don't use it for your interpretation of the relationship. Instead, use the percentaging technique results to identify and interpret the strength of the relationship between the variables.

Understanding gamma

Gamma is a PRE statistic that can be utilized when both variables in a contingency table are measured at the ordinal level of measurement.

To understand gamma, you have to appreciate the following two concepts:

- Gamma utilizes *pairs* of cases.
- Gamma utilizes the *rank ordering of pairs of cases*.

The following simple example will help you to understand these two concepts. Imagine that you went to a Grade 1 classroom and asked the teacher to rate the 'intelligence' of three students (Jean, Dale, and Lynn) and you then asked students in the class to rate the 'popularity' of these students. If each rating was on an ordinal scale, you might get results like the following:

Table 7.1 Understanding gamma

Popularity	Intelligence		
	High	Medium	Low
High		Jean	
Medium	Dale		
Low			Lynn

This example uses the unrealistic sample size of three students so that you can easily see gamma's two basic concepts in operation. The first of these concepts is that gamma utilizes *pairs* of cases. This is an important point, since it is typical for us to think in terms of individual cases (as we did in calculating lambda). So if we need to think in pairs of cases, we need to write out the pairs. In our example the pairs include: Jean–Dale (J–D), Jean–Lynn (J–L), and Dale–Lynn (D–L).

To say that 'gamma utilizes *pairs* of cases' means that the statistic does not look at any of these cases *as individuals*. In other words, we are not interested in Dale's or Jean's or Lynn's intelligence or popularity. Instead, what we are interested in is the relative intelligence or popularity *of the pairs*.

With this in mind, we can examine the second concept: namely, that gamma utilizes the *rank ordering of the pairs of cases*. This idea contains three components:

* Examine the rank ordering of each pair on the independent variable.
* Examine the rank ordering of each pair on the dependent variable.
* Compare the rank ordering of each pair on the independent and dependent variables.

To appreciate these components, let us apply each one to our example:

Examine the rank ordering of each pair on the independent variable. To do this, we list the pairs and 'examine their ordering' on the independent variable. 'Examine their ordering' means identifying which partner of the pair is greater than ($>$), less than ($<$), or equal to ($=$) the other on the variable. Applying this to our example, we get the following result:

Pairs	Order on IV (intelligence)
J–D	J<D
J–L	J>L
D–L	D>L

These rankings come from comparing the individuals in each pair on the independent variable. For example, for the J–D pair, we see that Jean has 'medium' intelligence and Dale has 'high' intelligence—therefore, J<D. The same process is followed for each pair.

Examine the rank ordering of each pair on the dependent variable. To complete this task, we follow the same process as the previous one, except that this time we use the rankings on the variable 'popularity'. This yields the following results:

Pairs	Order on DV (popularity)
J–D	J>D
J–L	J>L
D–L	D>L

Compare the rank ordering of each pair on the independent and dependent variables. This final step requires us to take the information from the previous two steps and compare the results. The following table provides the results of such a comparison.

Pairs	Order on IV (popularity)	Order of DV	Comparison
J–D	J<D	J>D	Different
J–L	J>L	J>L	Same
D–L	D>L	D>L	Same

The only new information in this table is the last column, 'comparison'. Here 'comparison' means 'compare the rank ordering of the pair on the independent and dependent variable'. For example, the reason that the J–D pair is scored 'different' in the comparison column is that the rank orderings of this pair are different (opposite) on the variable 'intelligence' (IV) when compared to the variable 'popularity' (DV). On intelligence, J<D, while on popularity, J>D. The other pairs receive the comparison ranking of 'same' because the two pairs' rankings on the IV and DV are identical.

To review, then, you now have an appreciation of the meaning of the two concepts underlying the logic of the PRE statistic gamma. You know what 'gamma utilizes *pairs* of cases' means, as well as what 'gamma utilizes the *rank ordering of pairs of cases*' means.

Next, we turn our attention to how to create a PRE statistic using this information. This is done by examining the four features that all PRE-based statistics share.

Marginal prediction rule and E1: A marginal prediction rule is a way of predicting scores on the dependent variable without any knowledge of the independent variable. To apply this idea to gamma, you must keep in mind that gamma focuses on *pairs of cases* and *the ordering of pairs of* *cases*. So for gamma, the marginal prediction question translates into how to predict the *order of each pair* on the dependent variable.

In our little example, this marginal prediction rule question means 'what rule can you use for predicting the *order* of each pair (i.e., J–D, J–L, D–L) on popularity?' So imagine that these three pairs of Grade 1 students are in the hallway, and the first pair walks in with paper bags covering their entire bodies. (The paper bags are required because you must make your choice *without any information about other variables*. So in order for you to be 'blind', such information must be kept from you.) What rule do you follow to guess which student has greater popularity? Remember, this prediction process has to be repeated for each of the pairs.

The answer is you 'guess'. Now, this may seem odd, but what else can you do? You have no idea which one of the pair is more popular, since you are 'blinded' to any information about them, so all you can do is guess. So the marginal prediction rule for gamma is 'guess' (i.e., make a random selection).

If you followed this marginal prediction rule, how many errors would you make? (Remember, the answer to this question is E1—that is, the number of errors you make using the marginal prediction rule.) Well, since for any pair you have a 50/50 chance of being correct, then E1 will be *half of the number of pairs of cases you have to make predictions for*. Applied to our little example, E1 will be 1.5, since we have three pairs of cases, and half of three equals 1.5.

Relational prediction rule and E2: A relational prediction rule is a way of predicting the dependent variable when you have knowledge of the independent variable and its connection to the dependent variable. Again, since gamma focuses on pairs and their ordering, the relational prediction rule asks, 'what rule can you use to predict the order of pairs on the dependent variable when you know their order on the independent variable?' To make this question concrete, in our example this question asks, if you know that J<D with respect to 'intelligence', what rule can you use to predict this pair's order on 'popularity'? The rule you select has to apply to all pairs of cases.

In fact, there are only two choices for a relational prediction rule for gamma, and your task is to select one of the alternatives. The first alternative is 'always predict *same* order', while the second alternative is 'always predict *different* order'. The first of these rules means that whatever ordering every pair has on the independent variable, you predict that they will have the same ordering on the dependent variable. If J<D on the independent variable, then predict J<D on the dependent variable, and so on. The second alternative means that whatever ordering every pair has on the independent variable, you predict that they will have the *opposite* ordering on the dependent variable. (Note: For gamma, 'different' means 'opposite'.)

The question then becomes, how do you know which relational prediction rule to select? The answer is to look at the 'comparison' column of the table and select the more frequently occurring response. Let's do that for our example. If you look at the 'comparison' column, you see that two of the three pairs of cases have the 'same' ordering on the independent and dependent variables, while one pair has a 'different' ordering. Since predict 'same' order is most common in our data, then the relational prediction rule for this example becomes 'always predict same order'.

For PRE statistics, when we select a relational prediction rule, we might make errors. These errors are identified as E2. To determine E2, *you count the number of pairs of cases that do not follow the relational prediction rule.* In our example, two of the three pairs of cases follow the relational prediction rule 'predict same order', and one pair does not follow this rule (i.e., the J–D pair had a 'different' ordering on the independent and dependent variables). So for our example, E2 is 1. This means that if we applied the prediction rule 'always predict same order' to all of the pairs of cases in our data set (i.e., three pairs), we would be incorrect in predicting the order of one pair on 'popularity'.

Calculating gamma: One method of calculating gamma is to use the (E1 − E2) / E1 formula introduced earlier. If we do this for our example, where E1 = 1.5 and E2 = 1, then gamma for that table is 0.5 / 1.5 = 0.33.

Interpreting gamma

Gamma is a PRE statistic and, therefore, has a PRE interpretation. The basic logic of this interpretation is that described in detail for lambda. It starts out: 'You proportionately reduce your errors by _____ per cent . . .'. So the interpretation of our example gamma of 0.33 begins, 'You proportionately reduce your errors by 33 per cent . . .'.

For the remainder of the interpretive sentence, you need to remember that gamma compares the prediction success of using the marginal prediction rule (i.e., chance) to the relational prediction rule (i.e., using either 'always predict same order' or 'always predict different order') for *pairs of cases.* Applying this to our example, the interpretive statement should read, 'You proportionately reduce your errors by 33 per cent when you know the order of pairs on "intelligence" when predicting their order on "popularity", compared to predicting "popularity" order by chance.' This may sound a little awkward, but it accurately expresses what the gamma statistics you have calculated mean.

However, this PRE statement only speaks to the 'strength' of the relationship. You also need to say something about the 'form' of the relationship between the variables. The information about 'form' comes from whether the gamma statistic you have calculated has a *positive or negative sign.*

Now, using the method just introduced does not tell you what the correct sign of gamma is. If you use this method, *you have to put either a positive or negative sign on the number* after it has been calculated. To determine what sign is appropriate, you proceed as follows. If the relational prediction rule is 'predict *same* order', then place a *positive* sign on the gamma calculation. If the relational prediction rule is 'predict *different* order', then place a *negative* sign on the gamma calculation. In our example, the relational prediction rule was 'always predict same order', so the gamma statistic should be +0.33.

So how do you interpret the sign to give you information about the form of the relationship between the variables? If the sign is positive, then the interpretation is that the pairs of cases change in the *same direction.* If the sign is negative, it means that the pairs of cases change in *opposite directions.* Applied to our example, the statement about form would say, 'The order of pairs on "popularity" is the same as the order of pairs on "intelligence".'

A final note

This tune-up on gamma provides you with an understanding of how this PRE statistic works and what it means. Although you could calculate gamma using the method described, in realistic research situations it is impractical to do so. In any case, you are going to have SPSS do the calculation work for you.

Given your use of SPSS, your primary task becomes one of making a proper interpretation of the results provided. Remember that legitimate values of gamma can range between −1.0 and +1.0. Since gamma is produced from a bivariate table, make sure that your interpretation includes both 'form' and 'strength' statements.

LAB 7 APPLICATION

Learning Objectives

The following lab questions are directed at helping you translate the material in this lab and Section 7 of SPSS Essentials into concrete research situations. Specifically, this lab assignment challenges you to clarify your understanding of:

- Generating and interpreting lambda and gamma PRE measures

Data requirements

To conduct the analysis for this application, go to the website and download the data set 'GSS2001.sav'. This data set includes various kinds of information about a sample of Canadian citizens.

Instructions

For each of the following three pairs of variables, conduct a bivariate analysis that generates the *appropriate* PRE measure of association.

Fill in your crosstabulation results (just the relevant percentages rather than numbers of cases) in the tables provided.

Underneath each crosstabulation, provide a statement that describes the relationship (if any) between the two variables.

Part 1: How much do men's and women's occupations differ?

For many years, it has been noted that working women and men are highly differentiated in the types of work they do. Women traditionally were restricted to teaching, nursing, and other 'helping' professions if they were not filling less prestigious jobs like cleaning or waitressing. However, the occupational divide has been changing in recent years. Statistics Canada uses what is called the Standard Occupational Classification to classify the wide variety of jobs that people do into just eight broad categories. These categories have been further collapsed into four broad categories for the purpose of our analysis: managerial and professional; clerical; sales and services; and manufacturing/industrial/transportation jobs. Use 'occup' and 'sex' to determine whether or not there still were substantial differences between men's and women's types of occupations in 2001.

Table 7.2 Percentage table (sex of respondent)

Type of Occupation	Sex of respondent		Total
	Male	Female	
Managerial and professional			
Clerical			
Sales and services			
Manufacturing/industrial/transportation			
Total			

PRE statistic selected:

_____

Justification for statistic selected:

_____

_____

Statistical interpretation:

Form:

_____

_____

Strength:

_____

_____

Conclusion:

_____

_____

Part 2: Is paternal education related to that of their children?

Students of social stratification often note that one's upbringing confers many advantages or disadvantages in terms of money for a good education, 'cultural capital', and so forth. Think about your own life. To what extent do you think that your parent or parents influenced the fact that you are attending university today rather than doing something else? Did their expectations play a role? Did you model yourself after your father and/or mother? The family is, after all, the primary agent of socialization. With respect to education in particular, the status of the father is thought to be more important to children's own educational outcome than that of the mother, although this is perhaps changing more and more all the time. Use 'educatn' and 'feducatn' to examine the relationship between a father's educational level and that of his children.

Table 7.3 Percentage table (father's highest education level)

Respondent's highest education level	Father's highest education level			
	High school diploma	Communty college certificate	University degree	Total
High school diploma				
Community college certificate				
University degree				
Total				

PRE statistic selected:

_____

Justification for statistic selected:

_____

_____

Statistical interpretation:

Form:

_____

_____

Strength:

_____

_____

Conclusion:

_____

_____

Part 3: Do women (or men) tend to marry people older (or younger) than themselves?

Respondents who were currently married (legally or common-law) and living with their spouse (i.e., not separated) were asked how old they were and how old their spouses were. This allows researchers to determine whether the respondent is older than, about the same age (within one year) as, or younger than his/her spouse—also known as 'age heterogamy'. Determine the extent to which the difference in age between the respondent and his/her spouse is related to his/her sex, using the variables 'agediff' and 'sex'.

Table 7.4 Percentage table (sex of respondent)

Age Difference	Sex of Respondent		Total
	Male	Female	
Respondent is two or more years older than spouse			
Respondent is about the same age as spouse (within one year or less)			
Respondent is two or more years younger than spouse			
Total			

PRE statistic selected:

_____

Justification for statistic selected:

_____

_____

Statistical interpretation:

Form:

_____

_____

Strength:

_____

_____

Conclusion:

_____

_____

LAB 8
Correlation and Regression

▶ Tune-up

Scatterplots

Research data are organized into contingency tables when the independent and dependent variables are at lower (i.e., nominal and ordinal) levels of measurement. When data from both variables are at higher levels of measurement (i.e., interval or ratio), the presentation of data takes the form of a scatterplot. Figure 8.1 gives an example.

Figure 8.1 Scatterplot

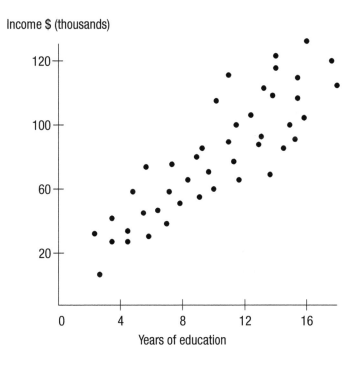

The 'dots' that are 'scattered' on the graph are the data on the independent and dependent variables for a set of 'cases' (i.e., subjects of the study). So the first thing to be clear about is that the graph that is the scatterplot comes from the data collection process.

Conventionally, the independent variable and its attributes are provided along the horizontal axis of the scatterplot, while the dependent variable and its attributes are presented on the vertical axis. In this format, you can see that each dot on the scatterplot represents the intersection of the independent variable and dependent variable. It is important to appreciate this observation, because it enables you to understand where the actual data that are represented on the scatterplot come from.

Each dot on the scatterplot represents an observation (i.e., some unit's score on the independent and dependent variables). To know where to plot the points on a scatterplot, you need to know the independent and dependent variable scores for each case (observation) in the data set. This information is provided in the form of ordered pairs. Ordered pairs are presented in the following general form: (independent variable score, dependent variable score). So if your age was 21 and you weighed 150 pounds, the ordered pair representing this information would be (21, 150).

Since a scatterplot presents information on a whole set of cases (observations), the information used to create a scatterplot is typically taken from a data set. To take a simple example, the following are the ages and weights for a set of five friends:

Person	Age	Weight
John	15	118
Samantha	23	145
Sigmar	28	210
Alice	49	152
Billy-Bob	89	185

To organize the data so that each case can be plotted on a scatterplot, they are transformed into ordered pairs including (15, 118), (23, 145), (28, 210), (49, 152), and (89, 185). If you plotted these ordered pairs on an appropriately labelled graph, you would get a scatterplot like the one in the earlier illustration.

Interpreting scatterplots

Once the data are plotted on a scatterplot, the question then becomes: what is the nature of the relationship between the independent and dependent variables? The answer to this question is found by examining both the display of the dots on the scatterplot and the best-fit regression line that is imposed on the graph.

An interpretation of the graph and the regression line is characterized in terms of three concepts: form, extent, and precision. We will discuss what each of these concepts means and then turn our attention to how to recognize each one.

'Form' on a scatterplot refers to the *structure or nature of the connection between the variables.* When you know the form of the relationship, you can make a statement about how the dependent variable changes when the independent variable changes in a particular way. In general, researchers try to identify one of four possible forms in a scatterplot: direct, inverse, curvilinear, and formless. The identification of a 'direct' relationship means that the independent and dependent variables change in the same direction. For example, as the independent variable increases, the dependent variable increases. If the form is identified as 'inverse', it means that the variables move in opposite directions. If the form is 'curvilinear', it means (as the term implies) that as the independent variable moves in one direction, the dependent variable moves in differing directions—sometimes increasing, sometimes decreasing. 'Formless' relationships mean that there is no systematic change in the dependent variable as the independent variable changes.

The form of a relationship in a scatterplot refers to the *underlying direction of change.* So to determine the form, you don't just connect the dots on a scatterplot. Instead, you look for the underlying pattern of the relationship. This is what the straight line on any scatterplot graph is meant to indicate. Lines on a scatterplot that indicate the underlying pattern are called 'best-fit' lines. If the form of a relationship is direct, the independent and dependent variables change in the same direction, and the line moves from the lower-left to the upper-right on the graph. If an inverse relationship exists, the direction of the straight line would move from the upper-left to the lower-right. In the case of curvilinear relationships, several patterns are possible, including u-shaped curves, inverted u-shapes, and others. In the case of formless relationships, the dots on the scatterplot are a random shape, which indicates that there is no underlying pattern (form) to the relationship between the variables.

The second concept used to describe the relationship in scatterplots is 'extent'. Extent refers to how much 'impact' changing the independent variable has on the dependent variable. Extent is a concept that only applies to direct and inverse (i.e., linear) relationships. To determine the extent of a scatterplot, you look at the slope of the best-fit line. The greater (i.e., steeper) the slope, the greater the extent (impact) of the relationship.

Notice that both form and extent of a scatterplot relationship are determined by examining and interpreting the best-fit (regression) line. The best-fit line, however, is a theoretical construct in the sense that few, if any, of the actual data points on the scatterplot may even touch the best-fit line. Look at almost any scatterplot containing a regression line, and you will see that this is the case. In other words, both form and extent give us a sense of what the underlying pattern of the relationship between the variables is.

Now let us draw an analogy. If you go into a shop to buy a new suit, the clerk will try to find a suit on the rack that 'best fits' you. (This best-fit is the equivalent of the best-fit line on the scatterplot.) Note, however, that just knowing that the suit (or the scatterplot line) is 'best-fit' *does not tell you how good the fit is.* (To draw another parallel, if your mother asks you how you did on the last course assignment and you answered, 'I did my best', your mother would not know how well you actually did. In the same way, describing the best-fit line on a scatterplot does not tell you how well that line actually fits the real data—which are the dots on the graph.)

This is what the third concept describing a scatterplot does: 'precision'. The precision of a scatterplot tells you *how well the best-fit line approximates the location of the actual data points*. The closer the data points are to the best-fit line (i.e., the tighter they are located around the line), the greater the precision of the relationship. In the case of perfect precision, all the data points fall on the line. From this extreme, the precision gets weaker and weaker until the points approach a random pattern.

In summary, without doing specific calculations, you can provide an approximate interpretation of the relationship between two variables contained in a scatterplot. First you look at the shape of the best-fit line and interpret its form and extent. Then you look at how well the best-fit line approximates the actual data and speak about the precision of the relationship.

Regression lines

With a best-fit regression line imposed on a scatterplot, you are able to interpret the general relationship between the independent and dependent variables. For example, you can report whether the form of the relationship is direct or inverse, you can report whether the slope is modest or steep, and you can indicate whether the 'fit' of the line is good or poor.

This is progress, but it still leaves two important questions unanswered: (1) where does the regression line come from? and (2) how are specific interpretations of form, extent, and precision made? These questions are addressed in turn.

Identifying the regression line: The dots on a scatterplot, as noted earlier, come from plotting the ordered pairs data. The ordered pairs, in turn, come from the observations of independent and dependent variable scores for each case included in the study. In other words, the 'evidence' on which a scatterplot is based is particular individuals' (cases) scores on two variables.

When a scatterplot is constructed, but before it is interpreted, a regression line that is 'best-fit' needs to be drawn on the graph. Imagine that you draw such a line on a scatterplot. If someone else were asked to draw the 'best-fit' line on the same scatterplot, it is very unlikely that they would draw the line in *exactly* the same location as you did. This demonstrates that different people will have different judgments about where the regression line should be drawn.

By definition, there can be only one best-fit line, where 'best-fit' means the *straight line that comes closest to all of the data points on the scatterplot*. How do we know where to draw this best-fit line? The answer centres on understanding the basic linear equation.

All straight lines are defined by the following general formula: $Y = a + bX$ where X is the independent variable, Y is the dependent variable, a is the intercept, and b is the slope. This equation tells you that the straight line between any two variables (X and Y) is characterized by a particular point at which the line crosses the Y (dependent variable) axis (called the 'intercept') and a particular slope (i.e., steepness of the line). You can demonstrate to yourself that this is the case by drawing any two lines on a graph. The only difference between these lines (assuming they are not identical) is their intercept and slope.

This appreciation means that if we knew the particular value of the intercept (*a*) and the particular value of the slope (*b*), we would know the formula of the straight line that relates any two variables. All that we would do is put the intercept and slope values in the general formula above, and we would have the specific formula defining the line relating the two variables.

This is not the place to enter a discussion about how the intercept and slope are calculated for any set of data. In most practical situations, including the ones in this lab, SPSS will do the calculations for you.

Imagine a data set that included respondents' self-reports of both their 'age' and 'number of friends'. If you ran an SPSS regression on these data, the output might report an intercept of −0.045 and a slope of 0.07. How is this information used to generate a regression line?

This question is simply answered by entering these particular values into the general linear equation. In this instance, therefore, the equation for the best-fit line relating age to number of friends would be:

Number of friends = −0.045 + (0.07) Age

Graphing the regression line

To understand what any specific linear regression equation means, it is helpful to draw it on a graph. To draw any line, you really need only join together two points. You already have one of the points that is on the line, and that is the intercept point. All you need is another point on the line. There are various ways this can be done, but a simple method is to solve the equation for any other value of the independent variable.

For example, let us take our equation (number of friends = −0.045 + (0.07) age) and solve it for $X = 50$. (That is, we are asking: if a person is 50 years old, how many friends do we estimate he or she has?) Putting $X = 50$ into the equation and solving it results in a Y value of 3.455. This result tells us that another point on the regression line is the ordered pair point (50, 3.455). All you have to do is mark this point on the scatterplot, put your ruler on this point and the intercept point, and draw a line. Following this procedure is exactly what SPSS does.

Interpreting the regression line

The 'form' and the 'extent' of a linear relationship between two variables measured at higher levels of measurement are obtained by examining the regression line. With the understanding you now have, you can make a precise statement about each of these features.

To speak about form, you can either (a) just look at the best-fit line you have drawn on the scatterplot or (b) look at the sign of the slope. If the form of the relationship is 'direct', (a) then the best-fit line will increase from the lower-left to the upper-right of the scatterplot, and (b) the value of the slope will have a positive sign. Alternately, if the form of the relationship is 'inverse', then the best-fit line will decrease from the upper-left to the lower-right of the scatterplot, and the value of the slope will have a negative sign.

To speak about 'extent', you need to remember that a synonym for extent is 'impact'. Impact is a nicely descriptive term that connotes how much difference something makes. More extensive relationships have greater impact. Extent is precisely measured by the value of the slope of the regression line. The greater the slope, the greater the impact.

Finally, remember that the interpretation of form and extent for any relationship is variable-specific and must use language that anyone can understand. For example, don't assume that ordinary people know what 'inverse' or 'slope' means; spell it out for them.

Interpreting the correlation coefficient

With the information from the best-fit regression line, you are able to identify and interpret the 'form' and 'extent' of the relationship between the variables in the scatterplot. The other characteristic of the relationship you need to speak about is the 'precision'.

'Precision' tells us how well the regression line fits the actual data points displayed on the scatterplot. The measure of precision is the Pearson correlation coefficient, symbolized by the letter r.

SPSS Essentials demonstrates the procedure for obtaining the value of this correlation coefficient. To interpret the result, you need to recall that r varies between -1.0 and $+1.0$. As r approaches zero, it means that the data points on the scatterplot are closer and closer to being randomly distributed. As r approaches $+1.0$, it means that the data points are more and more tightly clustered around a direct regression line. When $r = +1.0$, all the data points fall precisely on the regression line expressing the direct relationship. As r approaches -1.0, it means that the data points are more and more tightly clustered around an inverse regression line. When $r = -1.0$, all the data points fall precisely on the regression line expressing the inverse relationship. Unfortunately, there is no specific interpretation of the value of r. We are left speaking, qualitatively, of imprecise relationships (when r approaches zero) or of increasingly precise relationships (as r moves toward either -1.0 or $+1.0$).

It turns out, however, that when you square the value of r to create r^2, it creates a statistic with a PRE interpretation. This statistic is called the coefficient of determination. The coefficient of determination varies within the range 0 to $+1.0$. So, for example, when r is 0.7, then r^2 is 0.49. The coefficient of determination is a measure of the *strength* of the relationship between the interval or ratio variables. For technical reasons that need not concern us here, this measure of strength is a combination of the extent and precision ideas discussed previously.

One last point on interpretation: Since r^2 is a PRE measure, it is interpreted the same way as other measures in this family. For the age and friends example, the r^2 would be 0.669, which means that you 'proportionately reduce your error by 66.9 per cent when you know a person's age in predicting their number of friends compared to predicting the mean number of friends'.

LAB 8 APPLICATION

Learning Objectives

The following lab questions are directed at helping you translate the material in this lab and Section 8 of SPSS Essentials into concrete research situations. Specifically, this lab assignment challenges you to clarify your understanding of:

- Generating and interpreting correlation coefficients
- Generating and interpreting linear regression lines

Data requirements

To conduct the analysis for this application, go to the website and download the data set 'GSS1998.sav'. This data set includes various kinds of information about a sample of Canadian citizens.

Introduction

Not having enough time for essential sleep is one of the drawbacks of living in our modern, time-stressed society. In fact, survey research supports this notion. In 1998, Statistics Canada's annual *General Social Survey (Cycle 12)* asked respondents to provide details of how they used their time, including the number of minutes that they sleep per day (i.e., in a 24-hour period). Of course, some of us get plenty of sleep, while others do not get enough. Because chronic lack of sleep is thought to have negative long-term health consequences, it is important for researchers to understand what types of people are at relatively greater risk.

One risk factor is having young children. In this regard, you will be examining a sub-sample of the data: individuals with children who are all under the age of five. Your unit of analysis is the individual parent of one or more children under five (but no other children). Once you open the data set, use the variable 'children' and the Select Cases procedure to select respondents who have preschool children only (their value is '2'). You should have a total of 687 cases in your new sub-sample if you did the selection correctly. Your task is to explore one factor that might influence the amount of sleep that these parents get.

Instructions

1. Run and carefully examine frequency distributions, including descriptive statistics and histograms where appropriate, for each of these potential independent variables:

   'sex' (sex of respondent)
   'marstat' (marital status of respondent)
   'lfsgss' (labour force status of respondent)
   'workhrs' (average hours per day spent on paid work)[1]
   'chilcare' (average hours per day spent on child care)[2]

   Do the same above for your dependent variable 'sleep' (average hours per day spent on essential sleep/night sleep).[3]

2. Explain the methodological reasons why 'workhrs' is a more suitable independent variable than the others in terms of doing correlation and regression.

   _____

   _____

3a. In the space below, provide a hypothesis about the expected relationship between 'workhrs' and 'sleep'.

   _____

   _____

   _____

   _____

STOP

Does your hypothesis contain two variables? Is it clear, unambiguous, and testable? Is a direction (if applicable) indicated?

3b. Explain why you think that hypothesis is a plausible one.

   _____

   _____

   _____

   _____

4. To give you a visual estimation of the relationship, produce a scatterplot of your two variables. Based on your scatterplot, summarize the following characteristics:

   Form: _____

   Justification:

   _____

   _____

   Extent: _____

   Justification:

   _____

   _____

   Precision: _____

   Justification:

   _____

   _____

5. Run the Pearson correlation procedure. Provide your results and interpretation in the blanks below:

   My Pearson's r of _____ indicates that there is a _____ relationship between _____ and 'sleep'. Knowing an individual's value on _____ reduces our error in predicting 'sleep' by _____%. (Therefore the other _____% of the variance in 'sleep' remains unexplained.)

6. In the space below, show (1) how the r coefficient was translated into the coefficient of determination and (2) how you arrived at an 'unexplained' variance figure.

   Coefficient of determination calculation:

   _____

   Unexplained variance calculation:

   _____

7. Use SPSS to conduct a bivariate regression analysis of the relationship between 'sleep' and 'workhrs'.

8. Write out the general linear regression equation. Next, rewrite the equation for the 'sleep'–'workhrs' relationship by substituting the relevant figures from your SPSS regression output, as well as the names of your independent and dependent variables , in the appropriate places.

Regression equation:

_____

Regression equation for the specific relationship:

_____

9. In the space below, create a graph and draw the exact regression line on it. Does your regression line mirror the one in your SPSS output?

Graph:

Does your graph mirror the SPSS output? _____

10. Using the regression equation, predict how much sleep we expect to be reported by:

(a) Parents who work an average of 8.8 hours per day _____

(b) Parents who work an average of 2.5 hours per day _____

In the space below, show the calculations you used to make your predictions:

(a) For 8.8 hours of work:

(b) For 2.5 hours of work:

11. Suppose that a parent's physician was concerned about the potential adverse health impacts of their patient's time-stressed lifestyle and asked them to reduce their work hours in order to get 8.0 hours of sleep per night. Using the regression equation, determine the number of hours we expect they will need to work in order to follow this advice. Show your calculations.

Estimate: _____ hours

Calculations:

LAB 9
Inference and Chi-Square

▶ Tune-up

Descriptive versus inferential statistics

If you were to get a book on statistical analysis from the library, you would see that its content is roughly divided in half. One large section of the book would contain descriptive statistical analysis procedures; the other part would cover inferential statistical analysis procedures. It is important that you appreciate the distinction between these two types of data analysis.

In most cases when researchers collect data, they do not collect evidence from all of the objects in a class. When we want to know the opinions of adult Canadians, we gather evidence from a couple of thousand respondents, not from several million individuals. When we want to learn your blood type, we do not drain all the fluid from your arteries and veins. In other words, most data are collected from a *sample* of cases.

Sample data are typically what researchers have available to them, and when they *report on the characteristics of this sample data, they utilize descriptive statistics.* Descriptive statistics allow us to summarize and interpret the information we have collected from the objects in our sample. For instance, if we gathered evidence about students' quality of life from five different classrooms, we would use descriptive statistics to determine the average level of student satisfaction with their university experience.

Although researchers can study only the evidence they have in hand, they are really interested in the general case. We don't really care about the blood type that is evident in the drop of blood we collected from you; we are interested in the blood type of all the blood circulating in your body. Likewise, we are not so interested in the quality of life of a few dozen students (i.e., our sample), but instead our interest is in the quality of life of all students at the university. *To try to generalize from the particular cases we have gathered evidence on (i.e., our sample) to the general case (i.e., the population) is the task of inferential statistics.*

To this point, the labs have addressed descriptive rather than inferential statistics. You have used samples of data to address various types of univariate, bivariate, and multivariate questions. In this lab, our attention turns to some fundamental issues and techniques in inferential statistics.

The necessity of inference

The univariate, bivariate, and multivariate statistical techniques you have added to your statistical toolkit are of the 'descriptive' kind. They fall into this category because they 'describe' (i.e., report on) characteristics of the data collected.

The limitation of relying solely on descriptive statistics is that we *rarely collect all the relevant data*. When pollsters gather information about Canadians' attitudes or opinions on some subject, they certainly don't talk to all adults in the country. When professors ask questions on tests, they typically don't ask about every possible subject included in the readings and lectures. When a nurse wants to determine your blood type, he or she doesn't withdraw all the blood from your body.

As these illustrations indicate, the usual case is to collect data from a *sample* of the cases, rather than all of the cases (i.e., the population). This is done for all kinds of practical reasons. Taking this practical course, however, leads to the following problem: *We are not typically interested in the sample but rather in the population*. Pollsters and their readers want to know about all adult Canadians, not just a few; professors want to know what students know about all the material covered in a unit; the nurse wants to know what type all of your blood is, not just what type a single drop or two is.

This problem is addressed through inferential statistics. *Inferential statistics are a set of techniques for generalizing the findings from a sample to a population*. As such, they play a central role in the research enterprise.

The null hypothesis and the logic of inference

The goal of inferential statistics is to make a claim about *generalization*. Specifically, inferential statistics are calculated and interpreted in order to state the likelihood that the findings evident in the sample statistics (i.e., descriptive statistical results) are credible—with 'credible' meaning 'not the result of sampling error'. The logic of testing such credibility involves comparing two kinds of hypotheses—the research hypothesis and the null hypothesis.

The *research hypothesis* is just what the expression implies—the researcher's 'educated guess' ('educated' because it is informed by some theoretical idea and a 'guess' because it is a prediction) about what the results of the research may show. For example, in previous labs you worked with research hypotheses about the anticipated relationship between two variables.

The actual results of the research study are used to support or disconfirm the research hypothesis. This is what you have been doing as you learned to analyze and interpret data. It is always the case, however, that because the research results you are analyzing come from a sample of data (rather than the entire population), they may be a 'fluke' (i.e., due to sampling error). It is the task of inferential statistics to estimate the likelihood of such 'flukes'.

In order to make such estimates, the logic of inference requires that it construct an *alternative hypothesis* to the research hypothesis. This alternate hypothesis is called the *null hypothesis*. The null hypothesis is a prediction that there is *no relationship or difference* evident in the population. For example, if the research hypothesis expected that 'tall people consume more peanut butter than shorter people', then the null hypothesis would predict that there is no relationship between height and peanut butter consumption.

The reason that the logic of inference requires a null hypothesis in addition to the research hypothesis is a bit odd, since it involves 'double negative' logic. The key idea behind this logic is *that it is **almost impossible** to demonstrate that something is **true**, while it is **relatively easy** to demonstrate that something is **false**.*

This key idea leads to the following dilemma for researchers: *We want to demonstrate that our research hypothesis is true, but our tools are best suited for demonstrating that something is false.* The researcher's solution to this dilemma is as follows: *We state the exact opposite of what we want to demonstrate, disprove it, and accept the result as confirmation of our original idea.*

Let us translate this last sentence for you. What we 'want to demonstrate' is the *research hypothesis* (since this is our 'educated guess'). Therefore, 'stating the exact opposite' of what we want to demonstrate involves stating the *null hypothesis* (since the null hypothesis claims there is no relationship, when we actually expect one). If we were to 'disprove it' (i.e., disprove the null hypothesis), we would be declaring that *there is not no relationship between the variables.* No doubt you will be impressed by the awkwardness of the double negative statement. But you will remember that a 'double negative' is the same as a 'positive'. Therefore, by declaring that 'there is not no relationship' (i.e., that the null hypothesis is false), the researcher is actually providing support for the original, positive idea—namely, the research hypothesis.

Type I and Type II errors

Inferential statistics boil down to a matter of estimating the generalizability (from the sample to the population) of our research study findings. There is no way to do this without risk, and this uncertainty means that our estimates run the risk of error.

Basically, in inferential logic the researcher is looking at how different the actual sample findings are from what the data would be expected to look like if the null hypothesis were true. Based on this comparison, the researcher has to make a decision between the following two alternatives:

1. Accept the research hypothesis and reject the null hypothesis.
2. Accept the null hypothesis and reject the research hypothesis.

This decision, however, must be made under conditions in which the evidence is imperfect and, therefore, there is risk of error. The possibilities for error come in two types.

A first type of error occurs when the researcher rejects the null hypothesis when it is, in fact, true. This will occur when the researcher incorrectly chooses alternative 1 (above). This mistake is called Type I error. The second type of error occurs when the researcher does not reject the null hypothesis when it is, in fact, false. This occurs when the researcher incorrectly chooses alternative 2 (above). This is called Type II error.

To solidify this distinction in your mind, imagine a research question such as: Are there sex differences in social anxiety? Let us imagine that the researcher, for some theoretical reason, puts forward the *research hypothesis* that 'males experience more social anxiety than females'. For this example, the *null hypothesis* would be that 'there are no differences in social anxiety between males and females'.

The researcher collects the data from a sample of men and women and analyzes the results. After a consideration of how different the research evidence actually is from the null hypothesis (more on the actual techniques for doing this a little later), the researcher faces a choice about whether there are actually sex differences in social anxiety *in the population*. This choice involves selecting among the two alternatives listed earlier. The possible outcomes are as follows:

The researcher rejects the null hypotheses *when there actually are sex differences in social anxiety in the population*. In this outcome, the investigator makes the right decision (i.e., inference).

The researcher rejects the null hypotheses *when there actually are **no** sex differences in social anxiety in the population*. In the outcome, the investigator makes an incorrect inference and commits a **Type I error**.

The researcher fails to reject the null hypothesis *when there actually are **no** sex differences in social anxiety in the population*. In the outcome, the investigator makes the right decision (i.e., inference).

The researcher fails to reject the null hypothesis *when there actually are sex differences in social anxiety in the population*. In the outcome, the investigator makes an error in inference and commits a **Type II error**.

Statistical significance, Type I errors, and substantive significance

A cornerstone of the credibility of scientific research is being able to identify what is 'real' (i.e., being able to identify what is actually the case). For this reason, researchers *are particularly concerned about committing Type I errors*. The reason is straightforward. When a Type I error is committed, the researcher is claiming that something exists (by rejecting the null hypothesis) when, in fact, the thing (e.g., a difference) does not exist. These kinds of errors, if repeatedly committed, undermine the credibility of science as a method of knowing, since the method would routinely be telling people that things are 'true' when in fact they are 'false'.

One important task of inferential statistics is to determine the level of Type I error likely present in the data. In this task, inferential statistics calculate the likelihood that it would be an error to generalize the sample statistic (i.e., the evidence) to the population. This is the idea behind what researchers call *statistical significance*.

Statistical significance addresses the probability that the existing statistical evidence would have occurred by chance (and therefore is not a genuine reflection of what is evident in the population). By convention, researchers typically use 0.05 or 0.01 levels of statistical significance. In choosing these significance levels, researchers declare they are willing to risk that their research results are due to chance 5 per cent of the time (for the .05 level) or 1 per cent of the time (if they select the .01 level). The .05 significance level means that the results would occur by chance in only five samples in 100; the .01 level means that the results would only occur by chance in one sample in 100.

It is important not to confuse the concept of 'statistical significance' with the notion of *substantive significance*. Statistical significance only informs us about the likelihood that the results are due to chance (i.e., sampling error). This is useful information; however, it does not tell us anything about the *importance* of the empirical findings. When we refer to the 'importance' of the results, we are referring to 'substantive significance'. Stated another way, substantive significance is about how large the observed effects are. Note that aside from how large the observed effects are, whether these results are due to chance or not is a separate question.

To solidify this distinction in your mind, let us return to the issue of sex differences in social anxiety introduced earlier. Imagine that two different researchers investigated this question. Researcher 1 found that there were very large differences between males' and females' social anxiety, while Researcher 2 found small gender differences. Let us assume that both research studies reported that their findings were 'statistically significant' at the .05 level. This means that both researchers felt confident that their results occurred by chance less that 5 per cent of the time. However, although the statistical significance of these two studies is similar, the 'substantive significance' is very different.

Substantive significance speaks to how important (or, on the other hand, trivial) the research findings are. In Research Study 1, the substantive significance was high, while in Research Study 2, the substantive significance was low. In short, just because researchers report that their results are 'statistically significant' does not mean they are 'important'. Trivial results (substantively insignificant ones) may not necessarily be due to chance (i.e., be statistically significant), and it is also possible that important results (substantively significant ones) may be due to chance (i.e., be statistically insignificant).

Chi-square and other significance tests

Statistics texts contain all kinds of tests for statistical significance. These tests all use the same kind of general logic discussed here. There are various kinds of tests of statistical significance for different situations. In this lab, your concern is with one significance test called chi-square.

SPSS Essentials presents the procedures for conducting chi-square tests of significance. In interpreting the results of this test, remember that it follows the general logic we have presented. You start with a research hypothesis and examine the actual evidence collected to test this hypothesis in the table of 'observed frequencies'. Then you create a table of 'expected frequencies', which is a table of how the data would appear *if the null hypothesis were true*. Finally, you compare *how different* the table of expected and observed frequencies are, which measures how different the observed data are from the null hypothesis evidence. You then consult the chi-square table to determine how likely it is that you would expect such differences by chance, and in doing so you realize the level of significance of the findings.

LAB 9 APPLICATION

Learning Objectives

The following lab questions are directed at helping you translate the material in this lab and Section 9 of SPSS Essentials into concrete research situations. Specifically, this lab assignment challenges you to clarify your understanding of:

- The nature of null hypotheses
- The generation and interpretation of chi-square significance tests
- The nature of Type I and Type II error

Data requirements

To conduct the analysis for this application, go to the website and download the data set 'AFRO2002.sav'. This data set comes from a probability sample of South Africans.

Part 1: Is life better or worse after apartheid? Does it depend on whom you ask?

Between 1948 and 1994, South Africa was dominated by a governmental structure called 'apartheid', literally meaning 'separateness'. While a complex series of laws determined how the system worked, three essential blocks of legislation were: (1) The Population Registration Act (1950), which classified citizens according to one of four main racial groups: Bantu (black African), white, coloured (mixed race), or Asian (a number of humiliating tests to determine the race of individuals who were not very obviously white included putting a comb through a person's hair; if it got stuck, that person was identified as black); (2) The Mixed Marriages Act (1949), which prohibited marriages between people of different races; and (3) The Group Areas Act (1950), which relegated people of non-white races to live in certain areas (usually poor land).

Although many of them did not support racial inequality, South African whites enjoyed vastly better living conditions than blacks under apartheid, including access to good housing, education, employment, and income, and this division was promoted by the state. In his autobiography, Nelson Mandela wrote that 'Where one was allowed to live and work could rest on such absurd distinctions as the curl of one's hair or the size of one's lips.'[1] In 1994, after decades as a political prisoner, Mandela became South Africa's first black president following the country's first free general election. The more recent (and quite controversial) long-term president was Thabo Mbeki. Since the end of apartheid, the government has promoted more opportunities for non-whites. However, at the same time violent crime victimizing people from all of the different races has increased greatly. As well, most blacks remain impoverished and suffer a relatively low life expectancy because of infectious disease like HIV and other causes. Let's see how citizens of different races feel about the new South Africa.

Instructions

1. Run frequency distributions for 'aparthd' and 'race', and examine them carefully.

2. State the null hypothesis (H_0) for these two variables.

   Null hypothesis:

   _____

   _____

3. In SPSS, test your H_0 by performing a chi-square test of significance.

4. Fill your crosstabulation results into the following table. Take a moment to look at them, and think about what racial *differences* in opinion, if any, are demonstrated.

Table 9.1

Opinion on life since apartheid	Respondent's Race				Total
	Black/ African	White/ European	Coloured/ Mixed	South Asian	
Worse/much worse					
Same					
Better/much better					
Total					

5. Examine your chi-square test results. Interpret them in the form of a clear and precise statement.

   Interpretation:

   _____

   _____

   _____

   _____

6. It is not enough to simply learn how to recite numbers. As sociologists, we are most interested

in explaining patterns in social life. Based on what you know about South Africa, explain *why* you think you got the results that you did.

_____

_____

_____

_____

Part 2: Type I and Type II error

Any conclusion that we make about statistical significance carries at least some risk of Type I and Type II error because of the fact that we are making inferences about populations based on samples. We almost never know real (population) values for certain, because we rarely have the ability to measure entire populations. Instead, we rely on samples, whose values we hope reflect real population values very closely.

Instructions

Review your decision about what to do with the null hypothesis after you performed your chi-square test in Part 1. For each of the following two scenarios, circle a, b, or c to indicate whether or not that decision was made in error and if so, what type of error it was. Justify your selections.

Scenario 1: If in *reality* (the population), there was *no relationship* between the IV and DV, my decision constituted: (a) no error; (b) a Type I error; (c) a Type II error.

Justification:

_____

_____

Scenario 2: If in *reality* (the population), there was *a relationship* between the IV and DV, my decision constituted: (a) no error; (b) a Type I error; (c) a Type II error.

Justification:

_____

_____

LAB 10
Inference and T-Tests

▶ Tune-up

Three basic questions

If you look at any statistics book, you will see that it contains a wide variety of statistical proced-ures. Clearly, not all statistics are appropriate for every situation. The question then becomes: How do you know which statistics to apply to a particular situation?

For the most part, the range of appropriate statistical procedures can be identified by answering three questions:

- Do you want to perform a descriptive or an inferential analysis?
- How many variables do you want to analyze simultaneously?
- What is the level of measurement of your variables?

The answer to the first question leads you to statistics that either tell you about the sample on which your data are collected (descriptive) or tell you the likelihood of being able to successfully generalize your sample findings to the general population (inferential).

The answer to the second question leads you to analyzing variables one at a time (univariate), in terms of independent–dependent variable relationships (bivariate), or in terms of relation-ships that take other variables into account (multivariate).

The third question asks you to identify whether the variable(s) under consideration are at the nominal, ordinal, interval, or ratio levels of measurement. The answer to this final question complicates the answers to the prior two questions, since *different descriptive and inferential statistics apply to different levels of measurement*. This is why, for example, bivariate descriptive analysis using tables (i.e., lower levels of measurement) in Lab 5 used techniques that were different from bivariate descriptive analysis using variables at higher levels of measurement (Lab 8).

This same complication occurs in choosing appropriate inferential statistics. In Lab 9, you learned about the chi-square test, which was an appropriate choice when the bivariate relation-ship was in tabular form. This lab introduces an inferential test that is appropriate when the dependent variable is at the interval or ratio level of measurement and the independent variable has two nominal or ordinal attributes.

Understanding the t-test

There are various types of t-tests. The one considered here is the 'difference of means' test. The basic idea being tested with this statistic is that two groups are different, on average, on some dependent variable score. In this case the 'two' groups are identified as different attributes of an independent variable. They could be, for example, 'men' and 'women' in a sample or participants who 'were religious' and those who 'were not'. The differences on the dependent variable are differences in the 'means'. You will recall that the mean is a measure of central tendency best suited for variables at higher levels of measurement (interval or ratio).

In short, the t-test measures whether the difference between means of two groups are statistically significant. For example, it could be the difference in mean incomes of men and women, or it could be the difference in education among religious and non-religious persons.

Remember that the t-test is an inferential statistic, which means that it tests whether differences between the groups observed in a sample (the descriptive statistics) are likely to be found in the population. The null hypothesis being tested is that whatever the differences observed in the sample, there are *no differences* between the groups in the population. In other words, if the null hypothesis is confirmed, then the conclusion is that the observed differences in the sample are a result of sampling error and therefore are not generalizable to the population.

In the t-test, if the null hypothesis is rejected, then one can conclude (with a reasonable degree of certainty) that the descriptive differences observed in the sample are reflective of the differences found in the population. The 'degree of certainty' of such a generalization is associated with the confidence level.

LAB 10 APPLICATION

Learning Objectives

The following lab questions are directed at helping you translate the material in this lab and Section 9 of SPSS Essentials into concrete research situations. Specifically, this lab assignment challenges you to clarify your understanding of:

- Generating and interpreting the difference of means test
- Appreciating what kinds of problems are appropriate for t-testing

Part 1: Data requirements

To conduct the analysis for this application, go to the website and download the data set 'censusbaby.sav'. This data set comes from a probability sample of Canadians.

Instructions

1. From the data set, select only those persons who had either a maximum high school education level or a university degree. (In other words, exclude from your analysis respondents who had some post-secondary education but no degree.)

2. Use SPSS to conduct a t-test related to the question: Does personal income differ by education level? In this case, 'totincp' is the dependent variable, and 'keducats' is the independent variable.

3. For your test, what is the null hypothesis?

   _____

   _____

4. What is the mean income level for the two groups under consideration?

   Maximum high school education: $_____

   University degree: $_____

5. Are the differences between the two groups statistically significant? _____

   Justify your answer:

   _____

   _____

6. In everyday language, write a statement that reports what your inferential test says about the differences in income between education levels.

   _____

   _____

7. What is the probability that your generalization in this exercise is incorrect?

   _____

   Justify this conclusion:

   _____

   _____

8. In drawing your conclusion, what type of error are you at risk of making?

   _____

   Justify this conclusion:

   _____

   _____

Part 2: Data requirements

To conduct the analysis for this application, go to the website and download the data set 'areastudy.sav'. This data set comes from a sample of cities in North America.

Instructions

1. Review the variables in the data set, and select two variables that are appropriate for conducting a t-test.

2. What is the research question that links the two variables you have selected?

3. Generate a hypothesis that expresses a plausible connection between the two variables you have selected.

Independent variable: _____

Dependent variable: _____

Hypothesis:

_____

Justification:

_____

_____

4. What is the null hypothesis under consideration in this test?

Null hypothesis: _____

Rationale:

_____

_____

5. Conduct a difference of means t-test for your hypothesis.

6. What is the mean dependent variable score for the two groups under consideration?

Group 1: _____

Group 2: _____

7. Are the differences between the two groups statistically significant? _____

Justify your answer:

_____

_____

8. In everyday language, write a statement that reports what your inferential test says about the differences between the means of the two groups.

_____

_____

9. What is the probability that your generalization in this exercise is incorrect?

_____

_____

Justify this conclusion:

_____

_____

10. In drawing your conclusion, what type of error are you at risk of making?

_____

_____

Justify this conclusion:

_____

_____

LAB 11
Samples and Inferences

▶ Tune-up

Generalization

The inferential statistics in Labs 9 and 10 are concerned with generalization from the results found in a sample to the likely situation in the population. The logic of inferential statistics assumes that the sample data are from a probability sample. If the findings are from a non-probability sample, then conventional inferential procedures do not apply.

The idea of a probability sample is that you select cases from a population in such a way that the sample is a good approximation of the population. The sample results are typically imperfect for reasons related to sampling error.

To appreciate the notion of sampling error, imagine that we drew a random sample of 500 from your university and calculated the mean grade point average. If we conducted the sample properly, there is a strong likelihood that the average in our sample would reflect the typical grade point average among all students at your university. However, there is *some chance* that even using the best sampling technique, we will randomly select the 500 best performing students on your campus. Note that in this scenario, we do not know we have selected the 500 best performing students; we expect we have selected a typical cross-section of students.

If we calculated the grade point average of these 500 top performers (thinking they were typical) and then concluded that their academic achievement reflected the entire university population, we would be mistaken. Such mistakes in generalization are due to sampling error.

In this scenario, sampling error would not be confined to simply selecting the top 500 students. Sampling error would creep into our generalizations any time the sample result was an imperfect reflection of the population result. In other words, sampling error occurs in degrees; sometimes we are likely to be very wrong, sometimes somewhat wrong, sometimes very little wrong in our generalizations.

Sampling distributions

The typical research study relies on a single sample. In the scenario above, we took one random sample of 500 students from your campus. But let's imagine that we took another random sample of the same size and calculated the mean grade point average. It would probably be different from the previous one and, in all likelihood, closer to the real population mean. (After all, there is an infinitesimally small chance of randomly selecting the 500 top achievers *twice in a row*!) And if you conducted a third study of the same sample size, the mean estimate would be different again.

Imagine that every time you conducted such a sample and calculated the mean grade point average, you plotted it on a graph. If you repeated this process over and over, you would begin creating a sampling distribution.

A sampling distribution is a distribution (frequency distribution or graph) of a sample statistic (in this case, the mean) of an infinite number of samples of a given size. The sampling distribution is a theoretical distribution, since nobody ever conducts the same study an infinite number of times.

Even though a sampling distribution is theoretical, it has some very important and powerful properties. Note that the sampling distribution is a *variable*—that is, it is the number of times a particular result occurs across an infinite number of samples. Because it is a variable, the sampling distribution can be analyzed in terms of univariate statistics.

A first important point about sampling distributions is that they are *normal distributions*. Think about what this statement says. If you take samples and plot the statistic of a variable (e.g., the mean), the larger the number of samples in the plot, the more normal the shape of the distribution. This proposition (related to what is called the Central Limit Theorem) holds true even if the original variable is not normally distributed.

Beyond normality, a sampling distribution has a second major characteristic. This is that the *mean of the sampling distribution approximates the mean of the population*. Let that point sink in. Even though we don't know what the result is in a population (if we did, why would we bother to conduct research?), we can establish that result through reference to a sampling distribution.

A third major characteristic of sampling distributions is that as the sample size increases, the sampling distribution more quickly approximates a normal distribution.

Implications for inference

The features of a theoretical sampling distribution are powerful when married with actual research situations. Remember that the sampling distribution represents *all possible sampling results*. Any specific research situation represents one particular result. Put together, we know that the results of any particular research study are located *somewhere on the sampling distribution*. Given the normal shape of the sampling distribution, we know it is more likely that our specific research results will be closer to the mean of the sampling distribution rather than farther away. Moreover, sampling distributions are used to estimate the likelihood that a specific set of research results reflect the population result. These estimates are what the confidence level in an inferential analysis tells you.

LAB 11 APPLICATION

Learning Objectives

The following lab questions are directed at helping you translate the material in this lab and Section 10 of SPSS Essentials into concrete research situations. Specifically, this lab assignment challenges you to clarify your understanding of:

- How sampling distributions of repeated samples approximate normality
- How increasing sample size reduces sampling error

Part 1: The dice roll experiment

A sampling distribution is a theoretical distribution of all possible outcomes for a statistic. It is 'theoretical' in the sense that it is based on the notion of an infinite number of samples. Think about the roll of a fair-sided (i.e., not 'rigged') die. Each roll can be considered an *independent* sample, because one roll does not affect the next. Therefore, the probability of rolling a 1, 2, 3, 4, 5, or 6 is always one in six. The probability of rolling an *even* number of dots is one in two (or 50 per cent), because half of a die's sides are even numbered; 50 per cent is therefore our *known parameter*. If you rolled six dice at once, your best guess is that the mean will be three (i.e., 3/6, or 50 per cent, even).

In the following application, since we know what the population value is, we can see how closely our samples reflect that parameter of 50 per cent if we conduct repeated samples using six dice.

Instructions

1. Go to the book website, and click on the Dice Roll Simulator icon.

2. Enter the number 6 in the box. Press the Roll Them! button 100 times. You will effectively be rolling six dice, 100 times (i.e., 100 trials).

3. At the bottom of the screen, you will see that a second window has been created, which contains the results of your dice rolls. For each trial, in the 'Outcome' column below, record the total number of sides that have an even number of dots. (This number will range from 0 to 6.) Tip: To make your output easier to follow, you might want to roll the dice in batches of 10 or 20, deleting your previous batch once you have recorded your results.

Table 11.1

Trial	Outcome	Trial	Outcome	Trial	Outcome	Trial	Outcome	Trial	Outcome
1		21		41		61		81	
2		22		42		62		82	
3		23		43		63		83	
4		24		44		64		84	
5		25		45		65		85	
6		26		46		66		86	
7		27		47		67		87	
8		28		48		68		88	
9		29		49		69		89	
10		30		50		70		90	
11		31		51		71		91	
12		32		52		72		92	
13		33		53		73		93	
14		34		54		74		94	
15		35		55		75		95	
16		36		56		76		96	
17		37		57		77		97	
18		38		58		78		98	
19		39		59		79		99	
20		40		60		80		100	

4. Go to SPSS and create a variable called 'outcome'. Give it 0 decimal places and a variable label (e.g., 'number of even sides'), but don't worry about such things as defining missing values.

5. Enter your results for 'outcome', but for your *first five trials only*.

6. Produce a frequency distribution (including a histogram) of 'outcome'.

7. Enter your results for *your next five trials*, and repeat step 6 (i.e., you will end up with a total of *10 cases* in your SPSS data set and frequency results).

8. Enter your results for *your next 10 trials*, and repeat step 6 (i.e., you will end up with a total of *20 cases* in your SPSS data set and frequency results).

9. Enter your results for *your next 40 trials*, and repeat step 6 (i.e., you will end up with a total of *60 cases* in your SPSS data set and frequency results).

10. Enter your results for *your next 40 trials*, and repeat step 6 (i.e., you will end up with a total of *100 cases* in your SPSS data set and frequency results).

11. To spare you the tedium of rolling the dice any more but to increase your number of trials, below are the results of 150 additional trials. Enter the results for these additional trials into your data base so that you end up with a total of *250 cases* in your SPSS data set. Repeat step 6.

Table 11.2 Outcomes for another 150 trials

1	3	1	1	0	3	3	5
4	4	3	3	2	4	4	6
3	4	3	3	4	1	2	2
2	3	3	1	2	4	2	3
5	1	3	4	1	1	3	1
4	4	2	5	3	2	4	3
2	1	2	3	2	4	2	3
1	2	2	4	2	4	3	5
3	4	4	3	1	3	4	1
5	3	2	5	3	5	2	2
4	5	1	3	4	3	2	
3	4	2	1	3	4	2	
4	2	2	3	3	5	2	
6	3	3	3	0	4	3	
3	2	3	3	2	4	3	
3	2	2	3	3	1	2	
2	3	2	4	1	3	3	
4	3	2	3	3	2	4	
2	1	3	2	2	3	4	
5	4	5	3	5	2	4	

12. Examine your SPSS outputs for each of the runs. Below, provide a *rough* illustration of each histogram. Please don't worry about being elaborate; you just need to draw their overall shapes.

Figure 11.1

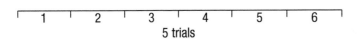

5 trials

Figure 11.2

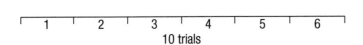

10 trials

Figure 11.3

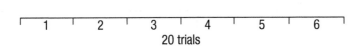

20 trials

Figure 11.4

60 trials

Figure 11.5

100 trials

Figure 11.6

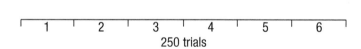

250 trials

13. What happens to the shape of the histogram as you increase the number of cases in the sampling distribution?

_____

_____

14. How does this result fit with the theoretical principles of a sampling distribution?

_____

_____

Part 2: The effects of sample size

Data Requirements

For this exercise, access the 2001 Census of Canada ('CENSUS2001.SAV') from the website.

Introduction

The creation of sampling distributions illustrates how accuracy will improve when repeated samples are tallied. In reality, however, we do not conduct repeated samples. However, we do make choices about sample size based on the notion of the sampling distribution, because increasing the *sample size* (*n*) has the same effect as conducting repeated samples. The larger the sample, the closer our statistic should be to its population parameter.

How can we test this aspect of sampling theory? Usually, our population parameter is unknown, because we are unable to survey every individual in a population. However, a census is not a sample but a complete enumeration of a population—i.e., everyone is surveyed—therefore, we know our parameter for this section of the exercise.

According to the 2001 Census, there were 15,300,245 females and 14,706,850 males in Canada, or 51.0 and 49.0 per cent of the population, respectively.[1] Our Census sub-sample contains 79,970 individuals randomly selected from the total number of individuals in the Census. Let's see what effect sample size has on the accuracy of sample values.

Instructions

1. Use the Select Cases procedure to take a random sample of five cases from the sample.

2. Run a frequency distribution of 'sex'. Record the female percentage in column 2 of the table below. Subtract that percentage from the known population parameter of females, and record the difference in column 3; that percentage constitutes your *sampling error*.

3. Repeat steps 1 and 2 but for increasing sample sizes (*n* = 25, *n* = 50, and so on). Record your results in the table provided.

Table 11.3

n	% Female	Sampling error (+/−)
5		
25		
50		
100		
500		
1000		
1500		
2000		
2500		
5000		
10,000		
50,000		

4. Suppose that you are working for the federal Liberal Party and for the purpose of adding statistics to a brochure, you want to know which party Canadians would vote for in the next election. You are able to include a question on an omnibus poll at a cost of $1 per respondent.[2] Your budget is unlimited, but you want to impress your boss with your cost-efficiency. Based on what you observed in answering question 3, what sample size would you choose and why?

Sample size: _____

Justification:

_____

_____

_____

_____

LAB 12
Putting It All Together

▶ Tune-up

Realistic situations

Different situations require different skill sets. In the previous labs, your primary tasks focused on applying identified statistical techniques to existing data sets. Using SPSS, you honed your skills producing and interpreting various univariate, bivariate, multivariate, and inferential statistical tests. Now that you have mastered these applications, we expect your feelings of competency have grown.

Now imagine a more realistic scenario than the ones you have experienced so far. In research offices across the country, whether in universities, governments, or the private sector, there are people just like you tasked with data analysis projects. And just as you have done in the experiences you have had so far, they are analyzing data sets.

But there is one important difference between your experience so far and theirs. In research offices, nobody tells the researchers what techniques are appropriate to the circumstances. You have had the advantage of working on labs that have separate themes. In the lab on correlation and regression, you knew what techniques were going to be applied to the data set. The same thing applied in the lab on univariate analysis and in all the others.

This final lab is closer to real-world research conditions in that it is based on a data set from a major Canadian city and challenges you to decide which techniques from your statistical toolkit are appropriate for answering a variety of questions.

LAB 12 APPLICATION

Learning Objectives

The following lab questions are directed at helping you apply the skills you have learned in the previous labs to a concrete research situation. Specifically, this lab assignment challenges you to clarify your understanding of:

- Conducting and interpreting appropriate univariate analyses
- Conducting and interpreting appropriate bivariate analyses
- Conducting and interpreting appropriate multivariate analyses
- Conducting and interpreting appropriate inferential analyses

Data requirements

For this exercise, access the Canadian City Area Study ('CITY2008.SAV') from the website. This data set contains a representative sample of 750 adults in a major Canadian city and includes a selection of the variables included in the original data set. In addition to the data set, the website also contains a codebook describing the variables in the file. You should download a copy of the codebook for consultation.

Instructions

1. Review the codebook for the data set, and *select a dependent variable* of interest.

2. From the codebook, *identify an independent variable* that you think might be related to the dependent variable.

3. *Develop a hypothesis* that predicts the way the independent and dependent variables are related.

4. *Choose a third/control variable* that might be expected to affect the original relationship between the independent and dependent variables.

5. Using the SPSS computer package, perform the appropriate statistical analysis to:
   (a) describe each of the three variables separately;
   (b) adequately test the bivariate hypothesis you have developed;
   (c) elaborate on the original relationship to determine the influence of the third/test variable.

6. Using SPSS, test whether the bivariate relationship is statistically significant.

Questions
Answer the following questions based on your completed analysis.

1. With respect to the *dependent* variable:

   What is the name of the variable you selected?

   _____

   What is the level of measurement of this variable?

   _____

   On what basis did you identify this as the appropriate level of measurement?

   _____

   Why did you select this as a dependent variable?

   _____

2. With respect to the *independent* variable:

   What is the name of the variable you selected?

   _____

   What is the level of measurement of this variable?

   _____

   On what basis did you identify this as the appropriate level of measurement?

   _____

   Why did you select this as an independent variable?

   _____

3. State your *hypothesis* of the expected relationship between the variables you have selected.

   _____

4. Provide a *justification* for why your hypothesis is plausible.

   _____

5. With respect to the *third/control* variable:

What is the name of the variable you selected?

_____

What is the level of measurement of this variable?

_____

On what basis did you identify this as the appropriate level of measurement?

_____

Why did you select this as a third/control variable?

_____

_____

How do you expect the relationship between the independent and dependent variables to change when the third/control variable is held constant?

_____

_____

6. With respect to the *univariate* analysis:

What measure of *central tendency* did you select for the *independent* variable?

_____

Justification:

_____

_____

Provide an interpretation of the meaning of the central tendency statistic.

_____

_____

What measure of *dispersion* did you select for the *independent* variable?

_____

Justification:

_____

_____

Provide an interpretation of the meaning of the dispersion statistic.

_____

_____

What measure of *central tendency* did you select for the *dependent* variable?

_____

Justification:

_____

_____

Provide an interpretation of the meaning of the central tendency statistic.

_____

_____

What measure of *dispersion* did you select for the *dependent* variable?

_____

Justification:

_____

_____

Provide an interpretation of the meaning of the dispersion statistic.

_____

_____

What measure of *central tendency* did you select for the *third/control* variable?

_____

Justification:

_____

_____

Provide an interpretation of the meaning of the central tendency statistic.

_____

_____

What measure of *dispersion* did you select for the *third/control* variable?

_____

Justification:

_____

_____

Provide an interpretation of the meaning of the dispersion statistic.

_____

_____

7. With respect to *bivariate* analysis:

What statistical procedure did you select for examining this relationship?

_____

Justify why this analytical technique is appropriate for the circumstances.

_____

_____

Interpret the bivariate statistics you produced.

_____

_____

Do the bivariate statistics confirm or disconfirm your hypothesis?

_____

Justify your conclusion.

_____

_____

8. With respect to the *multivariate* analysis:

What statistics were selected to analyze the partial relationships?

_____

What relationships were found in the partials?

_____

_____

How does the relationship found in the partials compare to the original, bivariate relationship?

_____

_____

From the multivariate analysis, what model best describes how the bivariate relationship is being affected by the third/control variable?

_____

Justify your selection of the model.

_____

_____

What does this model say about how the third variable is affecting the original bivariate relationship?

_____

_____

Does the multivariate analysis confirm your earlier prediction about the third variable's effects?

_____

_____

Justify your conclusion about how the evidence relates to your expectation.

_____

_____

SPSS Essentials

SPSS is a common software package used for analyzing data. SPSS stands for Statistical Package for the Social Sciences. The SPSS corporation produces several full-length guides for using the many sophisticated features of this program.[1] In addition, there are extended manuals available for using the common elements of SPSS .[2]

This introduction to SPSS is different. Our goal is to provide you with the 'essentials'—that is, the *minimum* amount of information required to get SPSS to perform basic analysis functions, particularly those required in the labs.

You could read the following material from start to finish and learn a lot. However, for current purposes, we recommend that you *read the sections when directed to do so in the various labs*. Each lab uses SPSS and directs you to read and utilize specific procedures. By learning and applying the analysis skills in a sequential manner, you will have acquired a useful working knowledge of SPSS after you have completed the labs.

Section 1: Getting Started

Starting the SPSS program

To begin, you need access to the SPSS program, either by purchasing a version or using a version resident on some public computer. The 'student version'[3] is relatively inexpensive and is commonly purchased by our students. Alternately, you may find SPSS in a public computer lab on your campus.

- *If you purchase SPSS*, you need to load the SPSS program onto your computer following the instructions that come with the disk.
- Next, *whether you are on your own or a public computer*, you need to open SPSS by clicking the *Start* menu (at bottom left of screen), finding the SPSS program, and opening it. Alternately, if there is a shortcut on the computer, you can open the SPSS program that way.

After opening the program, you will find that there are three main windows in SPSS. For now, we will be using two of these windows—(1) Data Editor and (2) Viewer (Output).

The Data Editor Window

This is the window that you see when you start an SPSS session. A Data Editor window automatically opens at the beginning of each new SPSS session. It has the title 'Untitled'. In this window you create or edit data. SPSS data files have the suffix '.sav'. In the Data Editor window at the bottom left-hand corner, you can toggle between 'Data View' (which allows you to view and enter the actual data) and 'Variable View' (which allows you to specify and view the variables) by using the appropriate tabs.

Figure 1 Data Editor window (data view)

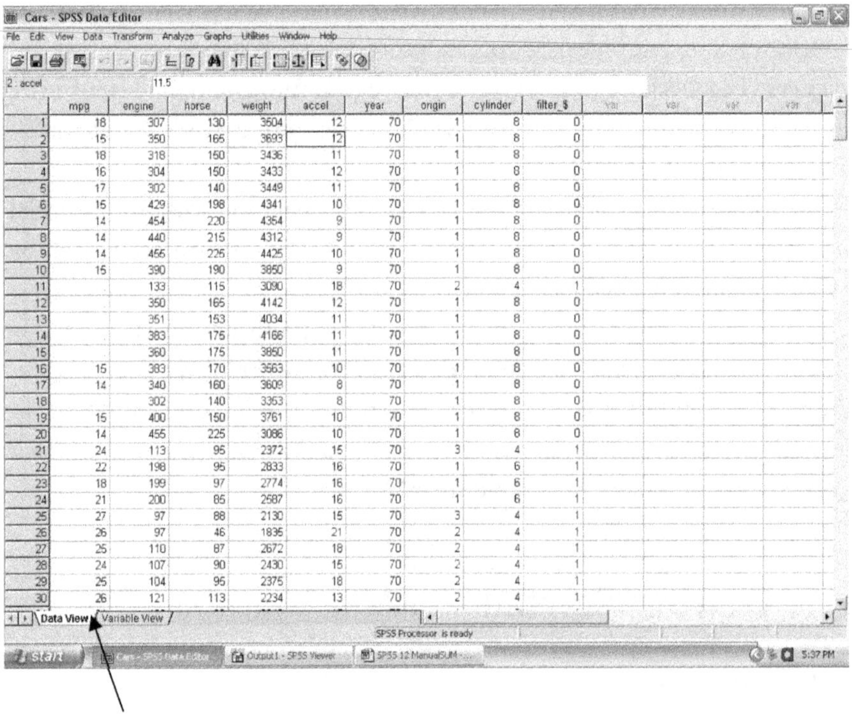

You can click on these boxes to switch from 'Data View' (showing values) to 'Variable View' (showing the specific characteristics of each variable).

The viewer window (output window)

This is the window where you see the statistics and graphics—the output—from the analysis work you performed using SPSS (e.g., pie charts, bar charts, frequency tables, crosstabulations, measures of central tendency). When you run a statistical procedure, the default output file is called 'Output1'. Your output can be edited here, just as you do with a word processing file. Keep track of your outputs during the session, since your outputs will be similar to one another. Output files have the suffix '.spo' or '.spv'.

Figure 2 Output window

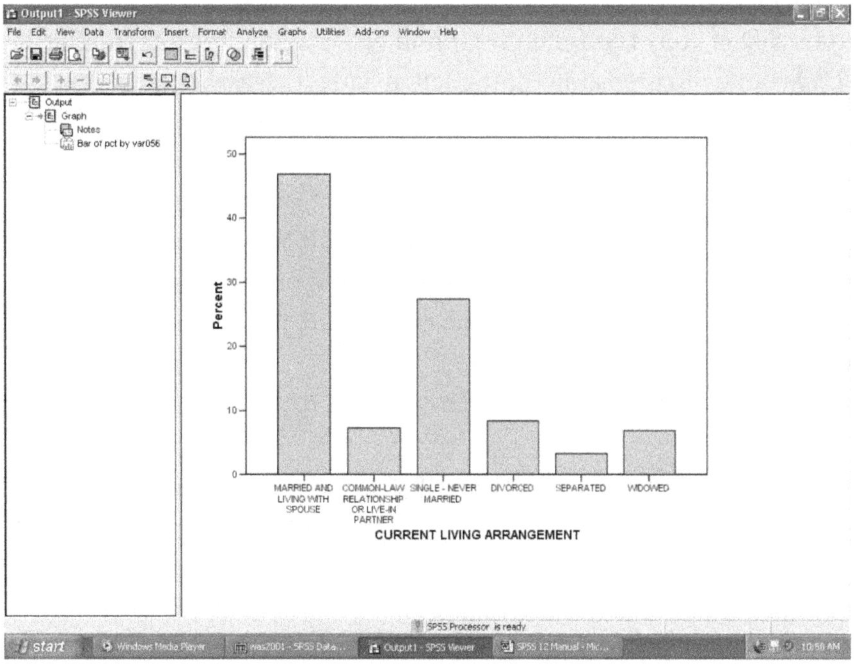

Setting options in SPSS

- Before opening a data set and beginning some analysis, you need to set some display options in SPSS.
- Go to *Edit* menu → *Options*.

  The *Options* dialogue box has a series of tabs at the top of the screen.

  The *General* tab should be clicked.

  Under the *Variable Lists* option, check *Display Names and File*.

  This will display the short names of the variables and arrange them in alphabetical order.

  You also want to set some options for displaying your output.

  Click on the *Output Labels* tab, and look at the setting under *Output Labeling*.

  Using the down arrow, you should select *Names and Labels*, *Values and Labels*, *Names and Labels*, *Values and Labels*.

- This will allow you to see both the names and labels of your variables and the codes and labels for your variables in all of your output.

Main Data Editor menus

Most program commands in SPSS are listed in drop-down menus. These program commands are listed *across the top* of the SPSS Data Editor window. Use a menu item the same way you would in any other program in Windows.

File: Used to create a new SPSS file, open or close an existing data or output file, save files, print files, and exit the program.

Edit: Used to modify or copy text from the Output or Data Editor windows. This is where you can use the *Undo* button to reverse an editing action and set display options.

View: Used to change fonts and view toolbars, status bars, and value labels.

Data: Used to make global changes to SPSS data files such as transposing variables and cases or creating subsets of cases for analysis. These changes do not affect the permanent data file unless you save the file on top of the original data. This menu also allows you to insert variables and sort variables or cases of the file based on the values of one or more variables.

Transform: Used to make changes to selected variables in the data file and to compute new variables based on the values of existing ones.

Analyze: Used to select and compute statistical procedures (such as frequencies, crosstabulations, t-tests, and chi-square tests).

Graphs: Used to create bar charts, pie charts, histograms, scatterplots, and other graphs.

Utilities: Used to display information on the contents of SPSS data files or open an index of SPSS commands. This menu is used to display information on the definition of specific variables, as well as complete dictionary information for the working data file or any other data file.

Help: Every window has a *Help* menu on the menu bar. *Topics* provides access to the *Contents*, *Index*, and *Find* tabs, which you can use to find specific *Help* topics. *Tutorial* provides access to the introductory tutorial. *The Statistics Coach* asks you a set of questions about your proposed analysis and then suggests a statistical procedure to follow.

Tip: There is no need to feel intimidated by all of this information. In fact, as the labs will show, you will be using only a small number of the wide-ranging capabilities of SPSS. There is a 'Quick Reference Guide' at the end of SPSS Essentials, which contains the procedures most frequently used in the lab assignments.

Opening a data file

* Data files for SPSS use the suffix '.sav'.
* The files can be accessed from any conventional source (e.g., SPSS, memory stick, internal drive).

    The files for these labs are available on the book's website, so you will need to download and save the data files as directed in the specific labs.

    Once the data file is downloaded and saved, go to *File* menu → *Open* → *Data*.

    This opens the *Open File* box.

    Look in → whatever location where you have saved the data file.
* Select '.sav' file → *Open*.

Key terms in Data View

Row: Each row is a single *case* (observation). For example, the data set displayed in Figure 1 measures the characteristics of a set of cars. The sample size includes 30 cases, each one displayed on a separate row.

Column: Each column in the data set corresponds to a single *variable*. For example, in Figure 1 the cars have been measured in terms of nine variables, such as 'mpg' (miles per gallon), 'engine' (engine size), and 'horse' (horsepower).

Variable: A characteristic or property of an object that expresses differences or can be changed (e.g., miles per gallon, engine size, horsepower, weight). Variables are represented in the data set as columns.

Value: The *responses* for each variable are called values, attributes, or scores. For example, the values for the variable 'mpg' (miles per gallon) are listed in the *cells* of the *first column* as 10, 15, 18, 16 . . . . Each value expresses a particular car's miles per gallon. The scores for each case's engine size are found in the second column of the table, and so on. Values are most often numbers, but not always.

Cells: Cells are the little 'boxes' that are evident in the Data Editor window. The boxes are the intersection of a particular row and column. The number recorded in each cell expresses the value of a particular variable (the column) for a specific case (the row). For example, in Figure 1 the first car in the sample (row 1) achieved 18 miles per gallon (column 1), has an engine size of 307 cubic inches (column 2), and so on.

Interpreting scores

The information presented in the Data Editor window is called a *data matrix*. By themselves, the numbers in the cells of a matrix are often meaningless; they require interpretation. Imagine that the cells of a column labelled 'ethnicity' contained numbers such as 1, 4, 6, 3, etc. What does it mean to say that an individual's ethnicity is '3'?

Interpreting the digits in a matrix requires a *codebook*. Sometimes data sets come with a hard copy of a codebook that allows you to interpret the scores of each variable. More commonly, you will need to retrieve this information from the data set. There are two common ways of doing this:

Creating a full codebook

You can have SPSS generate a codebook in the Output window for your entire data set. To do this from the Data Editor window:

- Go to *File* menu.
- Select *Display Data File Information*.
- Select *Display Working File*.

The results will take the form of the example in Figure 3.

Figure 3 Generating a codebook

Examining codes of a specific variable

If you want the *coding scheme* of a particular variable, proceed as follows:

- Go to *Utilities* menu → select *Variables.*
- On the left side, scroll down the list of variables until you reach the variable of interest.
  Highlight the variable name; its coding scheme (Value Labels) will be displayed on the right.
- For example, in Figure 4 we see that for the variable 'origin', a value of '1' denotes an American-made car.

Figure 4 Viewing the coding scheme of a variable

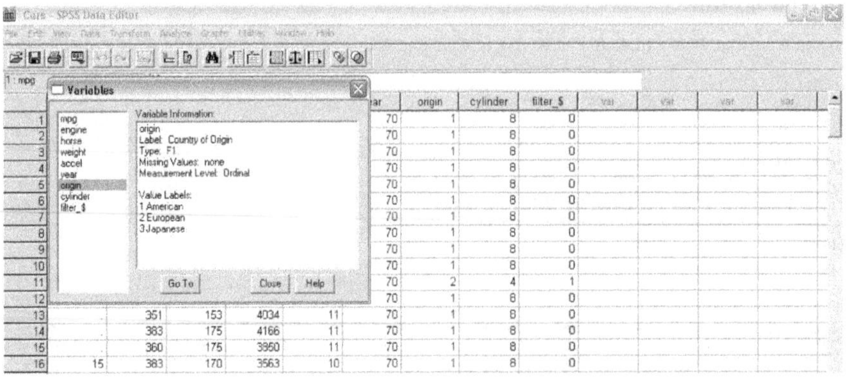

Creating or expanding a data matrix

Most of the data analysis exercises in the labs involve 'secondary analysis' of existing data sets. In secondary analysis, the data were originally collected by some other source, and you have obtained them for your own (secondary) research purposes.

In many research situations, however, you have collected your own data. In other words, you are conducting 'primary' research. In these cases, the data matrix is not provided to you; *you have to create a data matrix*. Creating a data matrix, or modifying an existing one, is a *five-step process*.

To appreciate the process, imagine that you wanted to add information to the matrix in Figure 1 about a sample of cars. In this case, suppose that you have acquired some additional information *on the first five existing cases* in the 'Cars' data set and would like to add this information to the existing SPSS data file. The additional information involves two variables, 'make' and 'model' of the car, and includes the following:

Make—The make of the particular car, with the following attributes: (1) General Motors; (2) Ford; (3) Chrysler; (4) American Motors; (5) Volkswagen.

Model—The model of the particular car, with the following attributes: (1) Belair; (2) Camaro; (3) Pinto; (4) Mustang; (5) New Yorker; (6) Gremlin; (7) Beetle.

Here are the values for your five cases. Note that the first case is a Ford Pinto, the second a GM (Chevy) Belair, and so on.

Case 1: 2, 3
Case 2: 1, 1
Case 3: 4, 6
Case 4: 1, 2
Case 5: 3, 5

Given this information, here is how you proceed toward entering data into an SPSS data file. Before you begin entering your data, you must *define* your variables. To do this you:

Switch from 'Data View' to 'Variable View' in the Data Editor window at the bottom left-hand corner (see Figure 1). Now you will see that instead of rows being cases and columns being variables (as was the case in 'Data View'), rows are variables, and columns contain the characteristics of each variable (see Figure 5).

As shown in Figure 5, you will see a number of columns, including 'Name', 'Type', and so on. For our purposes, we can ignore some of these columns. Instead, just focus on 'Name', 'Decimals', 'Label', 'Values', and 'Missing'. The steps involved in defining variables using these five columns are outlined below.

Figure 5 Data Editor window (Variable View)

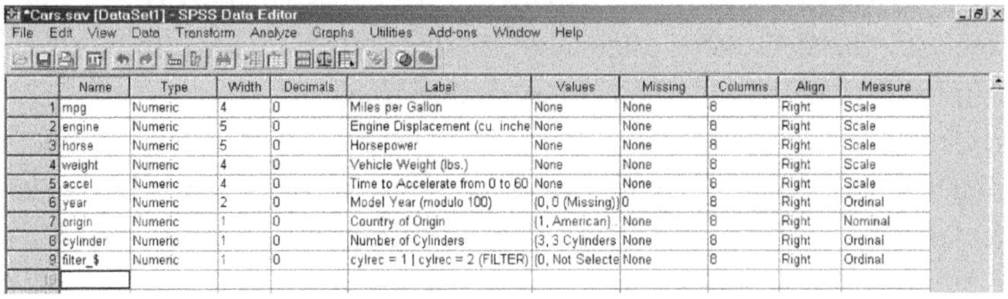

	Name	Type	Width	Decimals	Label	Values	Missing	Columns	Align	Measure
1	mpg	Numeric	4	0	Miles per Gallon	None	None	8	Right	Scale
2	engine	Numeric	5	0	Engine Displacement (cu. inche	None	None	8	Right	Scale
3	horse	Numeric	5	0	Horsepower	None	None	8	Right	Scale
4	weight	Numeric	4	0	Vehicle Weight (lbs.)	None	None	8	Right	Scale
5	accel	Numeric	4	0	Time to Accelerate from 0 to 60	None	None	8	Right	Scale
6	year	Numeric	2	0	Model Year (modulo 100)	{0, 0 (Missing)}	0	8	Right	Ordinal
7	origin	Numeric	1	0	Country of Origin	{1, American}...	None	8	Right	Nominal
8	cylinder	Numeric	1	0	Number of Cylinders	{3, 3 Cylinders	None	8	Right	Ordinal
9	filter_$	Numeric	1	0	cylrec = 1 | cylrec = 2 (FILTER)	{0, Not Selecte	None	8	Right	Ordinal
10										

The task of *defining variables* involves the following five steps:

- Step 1: Name the variable
  The first step in defining your variables is to give the variable a name of no more than eight characters, with no spaces. The variable name must start with a letter.
  Double-click the first blank cell that you see in the 'Name' column.
  Enter a name for your variable (e.g., 'make', 'model'). Many surveys use names like 'Var001' or 'Q1' for their variables, but you can use other formats.

- Step 2: Define an appropriate number of decimal places
  The default is two decimal places. Use the cell's arrows to increase or decrease this stipulation.
  For nominal and ordinal variables you can enter '0', because decimal places are usually not appropriate. For continuous interval/ratio-level variables, one or two decimal places are often appropriate (enter '1' or '2'). However, for discrete interval-level variables like 'year' (e.g., 1975), decimal places are not needed.

- Step 3: Define variable labels
  Although you may have given names to your variables, variable labels help us to better describe and remember exactly what each variable is about.
  Double-click the appropriate cell under the 'Label' column.
  Enter a description up to 256 characters long (e.g., 'make of vehicle').

- Step 4: Define value labels
  Normally, labels are attached to each value of nominal and ordinal variables. Without these labels, it is difficult for users of the 'Cars' data set, for example, to understand that a value of '1' means 'General Motors' for the variable 'make'.
  Click the Values cell in the row for the variable in question.
  Click the grey button in the cell.
  A dialogue box *Value Labels* will appear. In our example, you could assign labels 'General Motors' and 'Ford' to numeric values 1 and 2 respectively for the variable 'make'.
  Enter the data value in the Values box and its descriptive label in Value Labels.
  Click *Add* to record the value label for each data value and *OK* when you are done.

- Step 5: Define missing values

  When you do not have data for a particular case, you must specify how you will denote values that you want SPSS to 'ignore' when you run your statistics. If you do not do so, SPSS will include such values in calculations and distort your figures.

  For our 'Cars' example, we do not have any such cases; the notes below are just for the sake of interpreting future data sets that you will encounter in the labs.

  Any value may be defined as 'missing'. However, research conventions typically utilize the following: 7 = Not applicable; 8 = Don't know; 9 = No response/refusal (or, depending upon the range of the variable, 77, 777, or 7777; 88, 888, or 8888; 99, 999, or 9999). Make sure to give these values Value Labels as well.

  For example, a typical situation arises when a respondent refuses to tell us their income. This person would then be assigned a value of '999999' (we would not use '99', '999', etc., because these are legitimate values—e.g., a person might have an income of $999) For the variable 'income', unless you declare 999999 as a missing value, SPSS will think that this value means '999999 dollars' rather than 'No response', and your future calculation of mean income, for example, will be skewed much too high as a result.

  Click the Missing cell in the row for the variable → Click the grey button in the cell; a dialogue box *Missing Values* will appear.

  Select *Discrete Missing Values* (you can enter up to three missing values), and click *OK.*

Now that you have set up data entry specifications, entering simple numeric data is easy.

- Switch from 'Variable View' to 'Data View' by clicking on the tab at the bottom left-hand corner of the Data Editor window (see Figure 1).
- Select a cell for your first case (row) and newest variable (column); enter your value.
- Press *Enter* to record the value—or you can use the right or downward arrow keys or your mouse to move to the next cell.

Example: You can see that in our 'Cars' data file (Figure 6), the first vehicle (case) runs 18 mpg, has a 130 hp engine, weighs 3504 lb., etc., and according to our newest data is a Ford Pinto. (See the information before Figure 5 for a review of how to view a variable's coding scheme.)

Figure 6 Entering numeric data in SPSS

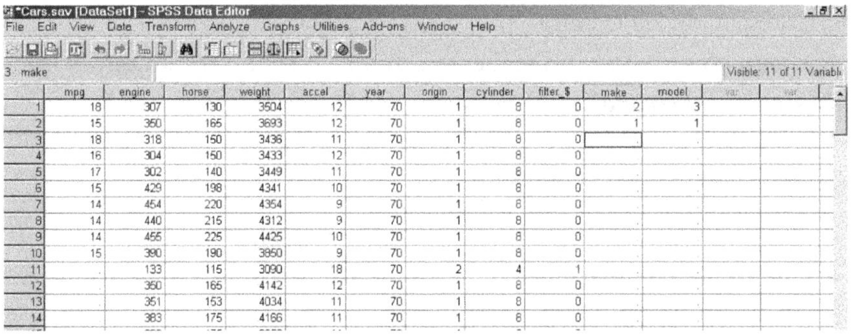

	mpg	engine	horse	weight	accel	year	origin	cylinder	filter_$	make	model	var	var
1	18	307	130	3504	12	70	1	8	0	2	3		
2	15	350	165	3693	12	70	1	8	0	1	1		
3	18	318	150	3436	11	70	1	8	0	.	.		
4	16	304	150	3433	12	70	1	8	0	.	.		
5	17	302	140	3449	11	70	1	8	0	.	.		
6	15	429	198	4341	10	70	1	8	0	.	.		
7	14	454	220	4354	9	70	1	8	0	.	.		
8	14	440	215	4312	9	70	1	8	0	.	.		
9	14	455	225	4425	10	70	1	8	0	.	.		
10	15	390	190	3850	9	70	1	8	0	.	.		
11	.	133	115	3090	18	70	2	4	1	.	.		
12	.	350	165	4142	12	70	1	8	0	.	.		
13	.	351	153	4034	11	70	1	8	0	.	.		
14	.	383	175	4166	11	70	1	8	0	.	.		

Saving files

Output (i.e., results of your analyses) and the data set are saved using the *File* menu. Saving files in SPSS is the same as saving word processing and spreadsheet files in Windows, although you must save changes made to the data set and the output separately. The roots for saving your file change according to the type of file you are saving. For example, '*filename*.spo' or '*filename*.spv' is an output file, and '*filename*.sav' is a data file. These suffixes appear automatically.

Procedure

- Go to *File* menu → *Save As*.
- In the dialogue box, name the output or data set. It is useful to name versions or use dates to differentiate files, especially when you are repeating actions many times or altering data sets over time. For example, if the same data set was altered over time, various versions might be labelled, 'was2001a.sav', 'was2001b.sav', 'was2001c.sav', 'was2001d.sav', and so on.
- Once you have named the file, save it to your hard drive or memory stick.

Exiting the SPSS program

- Go to *File* menu → *Exit*.
- If you have made changes to the data file and you have not already saved your data file, SPSS will ask something like: 'Save contents of data editor to C:\Program Files\SPSS\Cars.sav?'
- If you have made changes to the data that you want to retain, click *Yes*; otherwise click *No*.

Section 2: Describing Distributions

Producing univariate descriptive statistics

Univariate descriptive statistics provide useful summaries about the form, central tendency, and variability of a single variable.

Frequencies

The Frequencies procedure provides statistics and graphical displays that are useful for describing the distribution of a single variable. For example, imagine that you want to know: What is the distribution of males and females in a sample? If you use the Frequencies procedure, the output might inform you, for instance, that 41.3 per cent of your sample are males and 58.7 per cent of the sample are females.

Here are the steps you use to run Frequencies and its related procedures. Before you begin, make sure you are in the Data Editor window.

Procedure

- Select *Analyze* from the menu bar.
- Select *Descriptives* → *Frequencies*.
  In the left-hand box, scroll to and highlight the variable you want to analyze (for example, 'sex of respondent').
    Press the arrow button.
    Repeat the previous two steps to select any additional variables you want to analyze.
    Select *Statistics* box in the lower left-hand corner.
    In this menu, you can select your preferred measures of central tendency (i.e., mean, median, mode) and measures of dispersion (i.e., range, interquartile range, variance, standard deviation).
- Select *Continue* and *OK* to execute the Frequency command.

In the Output window, you will find the results of your analysis, an example of which is illustrated in Figure 7.

Figure 7 Frequency distribution in SPSS

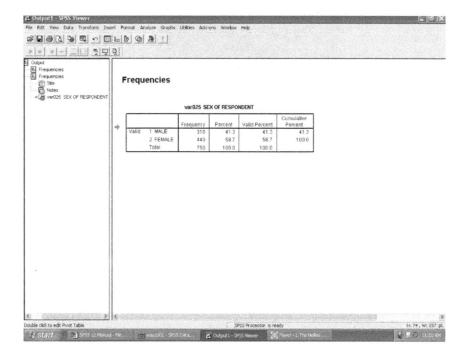

Graphical Displays

In addition to or instead of particular statistics, you can request that SPSS produce various kinds of graphs of the variables you chose. To do this, while you are in the *Frequencies* dialogue box (i.e., after step 3 in the procedure just described), select the *Charts* menu. In this section, you can select any of the three types of charts listed: bar chart, pie chart, and histogram. A bar chart displays the count for each distinct value or category as a separate bar, allowing you to compare categories visually. A pie chart displays the contribution of parts to a whole (see Figure 8). Each slice of a pie chart corresponds to each category of the variable. A histogram looks like a bar chart except that each bar represents a range of values. For example, a single bar may represent all people in their twenties. In a histogram, the bars are plotted on a numerical scale that is determined by the observed range of your data. A histogram shows the shape, centre, and spread of the distribution.

Figure 8 Pie chart in SPSS

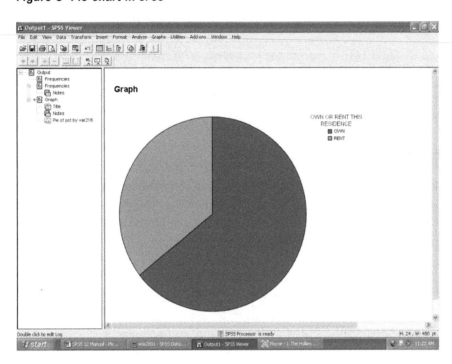

Section 3: Generating Standard Scores

To have SPSS create standard scores (z-scores) for any variable, use the following procedure. Make sure you are in the Data Editor window.

Procedure

- Select *Analyze* from the menu bar.
- Select *Descriptive Statistics* → *Descriptives*.
  In the left-hand box, scroll to and highlight the variable you want to analyze (for example, 'education of respondent').
    Press the arrow button.

Repeat the previous two steps to select any additional variables you want to create z-scores for.

- Check box entitled "save standardized values as variables".
- Select *OK* to execute the creation of z-scores for the variable(s) you selected.

Note: By following this procedure, SPSS creates a *new variable*. Each new z-score variable will be added as a column at the end of your data set. The new variable will have the same variable name as the original variable, except that it will have a 'Z' in front of it. For example, the variable 'Q15' becomes 'ZQ15'.

Section 4: Transforming Data

There are various reasons why you might want to modify your original set of cases and/or variables. Sometimes having simplified forms of a variable makes data analysis easier, while at other times you may want to add complexity to variables, such as the creation of scales. Regardless of your reasons, SPSS provides several data transformation options. This section reviews some basic data transformation procedures.

1. Recoding variables

The Recode feature collapses data into categories using existing variables.

Example: Suppose that you have information on each respondent's precise years of education. This is very useful information, since its high level of precision allows us to generate statistics like means and medians. However, suppose that you are really only interested in whether or not an individual falls into a relatively low, medium, or high number of years. The Recode procedure allows you to collapse the original education variable into three categories, using the following steps.

Step 1: Run a frequency distribution of your original variable

As an example, Figure 9 displays the frequency distribution for a variable called 'educ' (highest year of school completed). The output allows you to examine the overall distribution, as well as see whether there are any missing values. Often, the categories of new (i.e., recoded) variables are based on the number of cases that fall into a specific range; frequencies help to decide whether there are enough cases in each range to do so.

Figure 9 Frequency distribution of educ (highest year of school completed)

		Frequency	Per cent	Valid per cent	Cumulative per cent
Valid	0	2	.1	.1	.1
	2	4	.3	.3	.4
	4	7	.5	.5	.9
	5	7	.5	.5	1.3
	6	20	1.3	1.3	2.7
	7	26	1.7	1.7	4.4
	8	59	3.9	3.9	8.4
	9	45	3.0	3.0	11.4
	10	55	3.7	3.7	15.0
	11	81	5.4	5.4	20.5
	12`	445	29.7	29.7	50.2
	13	135	9.0	9.0	59.2
	14	166	11.1	11.1	70.3
	15	70	4.7	4.7	75.0
	16	208	13.9	13.9	88.9
	17	46	3.1	3.1	92.0
	18	71	4.7	4.7	96.7
	19	24	1.6	1.6	98.3
	20	25	1.7	1.7	100.0
	Total	1496	99.7	100.0	
Missing	98 DK	4	.3		
Total		1500	100.0		

After examining this frequency distribution, imagine we decide that there are enough cases falling between (1) up to and including 11 years; (2) 12 through 15 years; and (3) 16 or more years that we can create three separate categories. Other factors in our decision to form specific categories include whether or not they make logical sense. For example, it makes sense to combine people aged 20 to 34 and 35 to 44 rather than 20 to 32 and 33 to 36.

Tip: If you are doing a complex logical sequence of value combinations, you should consider initially writing out by hand the list of values that you want to combine via a Recode procedure; it makes the Recode task in SPSS much easier.

Step 2: Use the Recode procedure to create a new variable from the original one
Procedure
Go to *Transform* menu → *Recode into Different Variables*.

Select a variable (e.g., 'educ') from the list of variables and move it into the Input Variable → Output Variable box.

Select a name for your new variable (e.g., 'receduc' or 'educrec'), and type it into the Output Variable box. Under 'Label', a variable label can also be added at this point (e.g., 'education recoded').

Click *Change* button.

Select 'Old and New Values' button. This opens the *Recode into Different Variables: Old and New Values* dialogue box (See Figure 10).

Select the first 'Range' button under the *Old Value* dialogue box on the left; enter '0' in the first box and '11' in the second box. Enter the value '1' in the *New Value* box on the right. Click *Add*. This creates an educational range of 11 years and under, with a value of 1 for this new category.

Next, enter '12' and '15' in the same boxes that you used above. Enter '2' in the *New Value* box. Click *Add*. This creates an educational range of 12 through 15 years, with a value of 2. Do the same for the third category by entering '16' and '20', and enter '3' in the *New Value* box. Click *Add*. This creates an educational range of 16 through 20 years, with a value of 3.

Any other values that you have not included in your defined ranges will be moved into 'Missing', which means that SPSS will treat them as missing cases and ignore them in its calculations (see Figure 11). For our purposes, this approach is fine, since all non-respondents will automatically be declared missing; just be careful not to omit any cases that should in fact be in the 'valid' ranges.

When finished recoding, select *Continue* and choose *OK*.

Always run a frequency distribution of your new variable to see what it looks like.

Tip: Not sure what the highest value in the range is? Run a frequency distribution of your source variable to find out.

Figure 10 Recoding into different variable

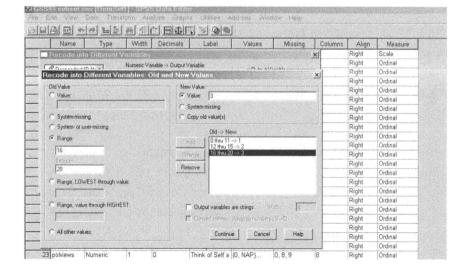

You should also give your new variable value labels via the Data Editor window.

After completing the Recode procedure, it is a good idea to run a frequency distribution of the new variable's distribution—just to double-check that the variable is now reclassified the way you intended. Figure 11 contains an example.

Figure 11 Output for education recoded into a new variable (categories)

		Frequency	Per cent	Valid per cent	Cumulative per cent
receduc Education recoded					
Valid	1 0–11	306	20.4	20.5	20.5
	2 12–15	816	54.4	54.5	75.0
	3 16–20	374	24.9	25.0	100.0
	Total	1496	99.7	100.0	
Missing	98 DK	4	.3		
Total		1500	100.0		

Step 3: Compare your original and recoded versions of your variable to ensure that you recoded things correctly

Compare the distributions of your original variable (e.g., 'educ') and your new variable (e.g., 'receduc') to make sure that all of the changes have been made correctly. For instance, count the number of cases in 'educ' that fall at or below 11 years; they should equal 306 (the total in 'receduc''s first category).

2. Computing variables

The Compute command can be used to create a new variable according to a formula.

Example: Suppose that you want to know each respondent's age, but the survey only asked their year of birth. We really want a variable for age, because it is more useful in terms of mathematical calculations (e.g., you can calculate a sample's mean age but not its mean year of birth). The Compute procedure allows us to create a new variable from existing ones, using the following steps.

Step 1: Try working out the problem by hand (create a formula)

It is often helpful to begin by working out the logic of Compute statements by hand to make sure you are on the right track. So in order to create the *new* variable 'age' from the *existing* variable 'year of birth', perform an example: how would you compute the current age of someone born in 1950?

The answer, of course, is to subtract their 'year of birth' from the current year (e.g., 2010).

Age = Current year *minus* year of birth

In our example, a person born in 1950 has an age of 60 (i.e., 2010 minus 1950).

Now that you have worked out how the new variable needs to be computed, the next task is to get SPSS to perform that computation for all cases in the data set.

Step 2: Use the Compute procedure and your new formula to create a new variable
Procedure
- Go to *Transform* menu → select *Compute.*
- Type in the name of your new (a.k.a. target) variable (e.g., call it 'compage').
   Click *Type & Label* to enter a description (under 'Label') of your variable (e.g., 'age computed from birth year').
   Click *Continue.*
   Put your cursor in the Numeric Expression box to construct the required formula.
   Type in your formula.
   Click *OK.*
- Your newly computed variable will appear at the bottom of your file in 'Variable View'.

Tip: You can also use the left box with its list of variables as well as mathematical operand buttons followed by the arrow button to input your formula if you find that easier than typing in your formula.

Figure 12 provides an illustration of the Compute procedure.

Figure 12 Computing a new variable

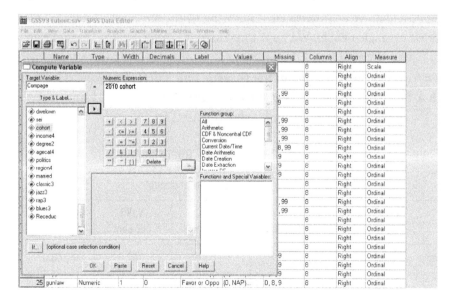

Other commonly used options include:

+ (plus)
* (multiplied by)
/ (divided by)
() (Grouping parentheses)

Step 3: Examine the value of your new variable for a 'test case' to ensure that your Compute formula worked correctly

Go back to a test case in the data set—say, a person born in 1950 according to variable 'cohort' (i.e., year of birth). Scroll horizontally to the end of the data set, and you should see that their value on your new variable 'compage' is 60, indicating that our Compute procedure worked correctly. You can see, then, that SPSS has subtracted every respondent's value on 'cohort' from 2010 so that we now have an age for every individual respondent.

3. Select cases

This command is not about transforming individual *variables* but about transforming the *sample* by selecting a subgroup of cases from the data file. Select Cases can be used to define the criteria of any subgroup, including: (1) separating out a sub-sample by a condition; (2) conducting a systematic random sample; and (3) selecting a specific number of cases but not randomly.

To Isolate a Sub-sample by a Condition

Example: Suppose that we are interested in knowing about the views of married people but not those of widows or single people. We want to exclude the latter groups from our analyses.

Step 1: Run a frequency distribution of the variable that will isolate your sub-sample
We first run a frequency distribution of marital status ('marital') and find that the value for 'married' is '1' and that 795 cases have this value (Figure 13).

Figure 13 Frequency distribution of marital (marital status)

			marital Marital status		
		Frequency	Per cent	Valid per cent	Cumulative per cent
Valid	1 married	795	53.0	53.0	53.0
	2 widowed	165	11.0	11.0	64.0
	3 divorced	213	14.2	14.2	78.3
	4 separated	40	2.7	2.7	80.9
	5 never married	286	19.1	19.1	100.0
	Total	1499	99.9	100.0	
Missing	9 NA	1	.1		
Total		1500	100.0		

Step 2: Use the Select Cases procedure to separate out your sub-sample

In order to separate out these cases (married people), we would use the following procedure:

- In the Data Editor window, go to the *Data* menu → *Select Cases*.
- Select *If Condition Is Satisfied* → Click If box.
    Scroll to and highlight the target variable in the left box (i.e., 'marital').
    Press the arrow button (▶).
    Select condition: = (equal to) and 1 (the value for married people)
- Select *Continue* and *OK*.

Figure 14 provides an illustration of the Select Cases screen.

A column titled 'filter_$' appears at the end of the data set. The 'Data View' confirms that the required selection has been made, with the case numbers of the deselected cases being crossed out.

Figure 14 Selecting cases by a condition

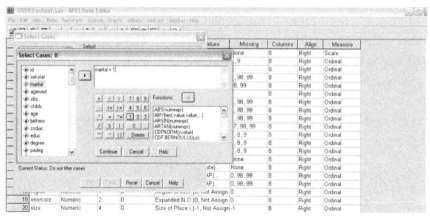

Other commonly used options include:

~= (not equal to)
< (less than)
> (greater than)
<= (less than or equal to)
>= (greater than or equal to)
& (and)
() (Grouping parentheses)

Tip: To remove the Select Cases filter, return to the *Data* menu → *Select Cases* → *Select All Cases* and *OK*. Once you have done this, delete 'filter_$' by highlighting the column and pressing delete.

Step 3: Run a frequency distribution to see whether you have the correct number of cases in your new sub-sample

To see whether your selection is correct, run a frequency distribution of 'marital'. Only the married cases (value '1') should appear, and you should have a total of 795 cases—the number of married people in the sample according to Figure 13. (In fact, you can run a frequency distribution of any variable at this point, and as long as you have a total of 795 cases, you will know that your Select Cases procedure worked.)

Section 5: Producing Bivariate Tables

Crosstabulation is a descriptive statistical procedure used for distinguishing the effects of an independent variable on a dependent variable. Because crosstabulation involves two variables, it is known as a *bivariate* descriptive statistic.

Crosstabulation consists of placing data for two variables in a contingency table (called a 'crosstab') to show the number and percentage of cases at the intersection of categories of the variables. Example: Imagine that you are interested in the relationship between sex (gender) and time spent with one's friends. From a crosstabulation output, you might learn that males spent somewhat more time with their friends—as evidenced by 41.4 per cent of males seeing their friends at least one to three times a week and 10.7 per cent daily or almost every day, compared to females' results of 33.6 per cent and 6.7 per cent, respectively. An illustration of the crosstabulation output is found in Figure 15.

When you are in the Data Editor window, here are the steps for producing crosstab tables.

Procedure

- Select *Analyze* from the menu bar.
- Select *Descriptive Statistics* → *Crosstabs*.
    Move independent variable 'Var025' (sex of respondent) to Column box.
    Move dependent variable 'Var059' (how often get together with friends) to Row box.
    Select *Cells*.
    Select *Column Percentages*.
- Select *Continue* → *OK*.

Figure 15 Crosstabulation in SPSS

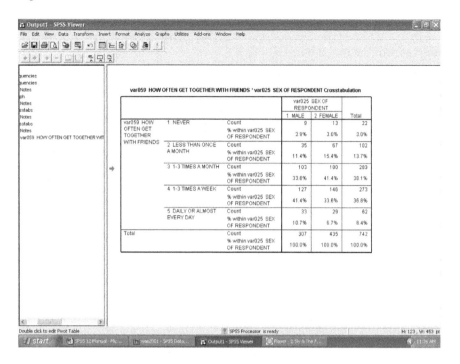

Section 6: Generating Trivariate Analysis

The previous section covered SPSS procedures for generating tables that displayed the relationship between two variables, the independent and dependent variables. These procedures were called 'bivariate' because the analysis included only two variables.

In order to determine whether a bivariate relationship is being affected by other variables, these other (third) variables need to be taken into account. For example, imagine that you were interested in the relationship between the 'minority status' of individuals (i.e., whether they were a member of a minority group or not) and their 'job category' (i.e., whether they did clerical or managerial work). This question could be answered using the bivariate analysis techniques you are familiar with.

However, let's imagine that you wanted to go a step further and ask whether the relationship between minority status and type of job is the same for both males and females. Now you have three variables in the mix—the independent variable (minority status), the dependent variable (job category), and a third (control) variable (gender). Trivariate analysis allows you to examine this issue, which can be reframed as the question:

What is the relationship between minority status and job category, controlling for gender?

Trivariate analysis uses the following procedure.

Procedure
- Select *Analyze* from the menu bar.
- Select *Descriptive Statistics* → *Crosstabs*.
    Move independent variable 'minority' to the Column box.
    Move dependent variable 'jobcat' to the Row box.
    Move control variable 'gender' to Layer 1 of 1 box.
    Select *Cells* → select *Column Percentages*.
- Select *Continue* → *OK*.

Figure 16 illustrates this procedure.

Figure 16 Requesting a trivariate crosstabulation

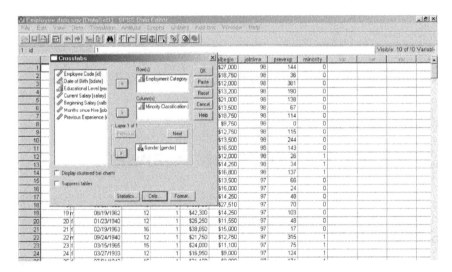

Following the trivariate procedure generates the output illustrated in Figure 17.

Figure 17 Output for a trivariate crosstabulation

jobcat Employment Category * minority Minority Classification * gender Gender Crosstabulation

gender Gender					minority Minority Classification		Total
					0 No	1 Yes	
f Female	jobcat Employment Category	1 Clerical	Count		166	40	206
			% within minority Minority Classification		94.3%	100.5%	95.4%
		3 Manager	Count		10	0	10
			% within minority Minority Classification		5.7%	.0%	4.6%
	Total		Count		176	40	216
			% within minority Minority Classification		100.0%	100.0%	100.0%
m Male	jobcat Employment Category	1 Clerical	Count		110	47	157
			% within minority Minority Classification		56.7%	73.4%	60.9%
		2 Custodial	Count		14	13	27
			% within minority Minority Classification		7.2%	20.3%	10.5%
		3 Manager	Count		70	4	74
			% within minority Minority Classification		36.1%	6.3%	28.7%
	Total		Count		194	64	258
			% within minority Minority Classification		100.0%	100.0%	100.0%

Notice that the output generates two trivariate tables. Each trivariate table has the same independent variable ('minority status') and dependent variable ('job category') as the original bivariate distribution. What makes it a *tri* variate table is that the table also includes the additional variable 'gender'. In Figure 17, there is one table for females only (the top half of the output in Figure 17) and one for males only (the bottom half).

Section 7: PRE Measures for Crosstabs

Section 5 introduced you to the procedures for generating bivariate tables. In that section, you learned how SPSS can produce percentages that supply appropriately standardized conditional distributions. In this section, you will learn how to analyze these same bivariate tables through different techniques—namely, proportional reduction in error (PRE) statistics.

Specifically, we will look at how the PRE measures lambda and gamma are generated.

Lambda

To calculate lambda in SPSS, the first step is to generate a bivariate contingency table to get a visual estimation of the relationship. Then we request the measure of association, lambda, which summarizes that relationship in a single number.

The following procedure illustrates the steps for generating lambda for the research question: Does the number of cylinders in cars differ by country of manufacture?

Procedure

- Select *Analyze* from the menu bar.
- Select *Descriptive Statistics* → *Crosstabs*.
    Move dependent variable 'cylinder' to the Row box.
    Move independent variable 'origin' to the Column box.
    Select *Cells* → *Column Percentages* → *Continue*.
    Select *Statistics* → *Lambda*.
- Select *Continue* → *OK*.

This procedure parallels the steps used to generate percentaged bivariate tables in Section 5. The only addition is the request for the lambda statistics to be calculated for the table.

Following this procedure will generate (1) a conventional percentaged bivariate table (see Section 5) and (2) a table called 'Directional Measures' in the Output window (Figure 18). Look under the column titled 'Value' to see the lambda calculations. In this column, you will notice that there are various lambdas, depending on which row you use. The first three rows under the 'Value' column describe different forms of lambda. The first row is a 'symmetrical' lambda, while rows 2 and 3 report 'asymmetrical' lambdas.

In most cases, one of the *asymmetrical* lambdas will be most appropriate. 'Asymmetrical' means that you can distinguish which of the variables in the bivariate table is the independent variable and which is dependent. ('Symmetrical' means that you are unable to make this distinction.)

In this particular case, we know the independent variable is 'origin' (country of manufacture) and the dependent variable is 'cylinder' (number of cylinders). Therefore, the appropriate lambda is 0.177, since this value uses 'cylinder' as the dependent variable.

Figure 18 Output for lambda

Directional Measures

			Value	Asymp. Std. Error	Approx. T	Approx. Sig.
Nominal by Nominal	Lambda	Symmetric	.120	.036	3.116	.002
		cylinder Number of Cylinders Dependent	.177	.061	2.638	.008
		origin Country of Origin Dependent	.046	.017	2.669	.008
	Goodman and Kruskal tau	cylinder Number of Cylinders Dependent	.225	.024		.000
		origin Country of Origin Dependent	.285	.023		.000

a. Not assuming the null hypothesis.

b. Using the asymptotic standard error assuming the null hypothesis.

Gamma

The SPSS procedures for generating gamma are similar to those for lambda, because both are based on bivariate crosstabulations. The Output windows (Figure 19) also look similar.

The following procedure shows the steps for generating gamma for the research problem: Does level of peanut butter consumption affect self-esteem?

Procedure

- Select *Analyze* from the menu bar.
- Select *Descriptive Statistics* → *Crosstabs*.
    Move dependent variable 'esteem' to the Row box.
    Move independent variable 'consumption' to the Column box.
    Select *Cells* → *Column Percentages* → *Continue*.
    Select *Statistics* → *Gamma*.
- Select *Continue* → *OK*.

In additional to a conventional percentaged table, this procedure will generate a table called 'Symmetric Measures' in the Output window (Figure 19). Look under the column titled 'Value' and the row titled 'Ordinal by Ordinal—Gamma'. In this case, the value of gamma is −.366. For current purposes, you can disregard the other information in the 'Symmetrical Measures' table.

Figure 19 Output for gamma

Symmetric Measures

		Value	Asymp. Std. Error[a]	Approx. T[b]	Approx. Sig.
Ordinal by Ordinal	Gamma	-.366	.047	-7.601	.000
N of Valid Cases		405			

[a]. Not assuming the null hypothesis.

[b]. Using the asymptotic standard error assuming the null hypothesis.

Section 8: Correlation and Regression

Section 7 covered two basic PRE statistics commonly used to analyze bivariate tables (crosstabs). These PRE measures were appropriate when the independent and dependent variables were measured at the lower levels of measurement (i.e., nominal and ordinal). This section provides the SPSS instructions for performing analysis between two variables that are measured at higher (i.e., interval and ratio) levels of measurement.

Pearson's correlation coefficient (r)

Lambda and gamma were rooted in bivariate tables. By contrast, Pearson's r is based on a scatterplot. Therefore, the initial step requires producing a scatterplot to get a visual estimation of the relationship between the independent and dependent variables.

Step 1: Produce a scatterplot

Scatterplots provide a visual impression of the form, extent, and precision of the association between two variables. To gain a sense of what the relationship actually looks like, you should always run a scatterplot before you request a measure of association like Pearson's r.

   For example, suppose we were interested in whether there is a correlation between the weight of a vehicle and the number of miles per gallon it gets. The procedure for producing the initial scatterplot between these variables is as follows.

Procedure
- Select *Graphs → Legacy Dialogs* from the menu bar.
- Select *Scatter/Dot.*
     Select *Simple Scatter → Define.*
     Move independent variable 'weight' (vehicle weight) to the X axis.
     Move dependent variable 'mpg' (miles per gallon) to the Y axis.
     Select *OK.* In the Output window, a scatterplot will be displayed (see Figure 20).
- To add a best fit-line: Double-click *Scatterplot → select Elements → Fit Line at Total.*

Following this procedure will produce a scatterplot in the Output window like the one in Figure 20.

Figure 20 Output for a scatterplot

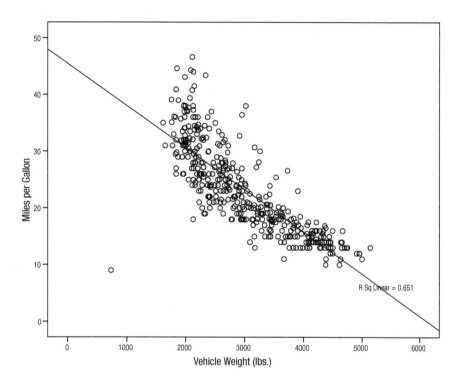

Step 2: Compute Pearson's *r* in SPSS

The scatterplot provides you with a visual representation of how the independent and dependent variables are related. The next step is to get an estimate of how well the line 'fits' the actual data points. This is done by generating the Pearson's *r* statistic.

Procedure

- Select *Analyze* from the menu bar.
- Select *Correlate* → *Bivariate*.

    On the left side, scroll down the list of variables until you find your independent and dependent variables.

    Highlight the variable name ('weight').

    Click the arrow button.

    Do this again for the second variable ('mpg').

- Select *OK*.

This procedure will result in a table titled 'Correlations' appearing in the Output window (Figure 21). Notice that the coefficients in this table appear as a matrix. In other words, the calculations include both variables as columns and as rows. For this reason, the Pearson correlation will be duplicated.

Within this table, examine the Pearson's *r* (correlation) for one combination of the independent and dependent variables. If we look in the cell in the upper-right corner, we observe that *r* = −0.807. For current purposes, you can ignore the information about significance (sig) and sample size (*N*) included in the cells of the table.

Figure 21 Output for Pearson's

Correlations

		weight Vehicle Weight (lbs.)	mpg Miles per Gallon
weight Vehicle Weight (lbs.)	Pearson Correlation	1	-.807*
	Sig. (2-tailed)		.000
	N	406	398
mpg Miles per Gallon	Pearson Correlation	-.807**	1
	Sig. (2-tailed)	.000	
	N	398	398

*Correlation is significant at the 0.01 level (2-tailed).

Bivariate linear regression

The Pearson's *r* correlation coefficient is a statistic that measures the 'fit' of a straight line on a scatterplot. The constants (intercept and slope) that define the line of best 'fit' are produced through regression analysis.

For example, demographers note that education, particularly among women, results in delayed childbearing and thereby lowered fertility. The longer a woman attends school, the later she starts having children. The later she starts having children, the fewer children she is likely to have in her lifetime. You might notice this in your own ancestors' lifetimes. Perhaps your maternal grandmother was subject to an arranged marriage at age 15 and began having children by age 16, ending up with nine in total. By contrast, many women today do not begin having children until well into their thirties, especially if they pursue a post-secondary education and career.

For a sample of women, linear regression can be used to determine which line best fits the data displaying the connection between education (the independent variable) and fertility (the dependent variable). The intercept and slope of such a best-fit regression line are determined using the following procedure.

Procedure

- Select *Analyze* from the menu bar.
- Select *Regression* → *Linear*.
    Place 'educ' (years of education) into the Independent box.
    Place 'childs' (number of children) into the Dependent box.
- Click *OK*.

Running this procedure will result in output similar to that in Figure 22.

The regression output contains a lot of information that can be ignored for current purposes. Of importance are the three pieces of information noted in Figure 22. In the table labelled 'Coefficients' are the intercept and slope. The intercept of the regression line is found next to the label 'Constant'. The slope of the regression line is found below the intercept in the column labelled 'B'. The Pearson's correlation coefficient is found in the 'Model Summary' table in the column labelled 'R'. If you are interested in the statistic that measures the 'strength' of the connection between the variables (the coefficient of determination), it is found in the column labelled 'Adjusted R Square'.

Figure 22 Regression output

Model Summary

Model	R	R Square	Adjusted R Square	Std. Error of the Estimate
1	.270[a]	.073	.072	1.696

[a]Predictors: (Constant), educ Highest Year of School

This is the explained variation R^2).[4]

This is the value of the intercept (a).   This is the value of the slope (b).

Coefficients[a]

Model	Unstandardized Coefficients		Standardized Coefficients	t	Sig.
	B	Std. Error	Beta		
1 (Constant)	3.950	.194		20.402	.000
educ Highest Year of School Completed	-.159	.015	-.270	-10.876	.000

[a]Dependent Variable: childs Number of Children

Section 9: Inferential Statistics

This section introduces two types of significance test, which are a branch of inferential statistics. These tests include chi-square and t-tests, and they are considered in turn.

Chi-Square

Chi-square (χ^2) is a non-parametric statistical test for categorical data and is used very commonly in the social sciences. You will often see chi-square statistics used when the data are in the form of tables. For example, imagine that you want to know whether or not the relationship that you believe exists between minority classification and employment category is statistically significant (i.e., how likely is it due to chance?). This question could be answered by conducting a chi-square test according to the following procedure.

Procedure
- Select *Analyze* from the menu bar.
- Select *Descriptive Statistics* → *Crosstabs*.
    Place independent variable 'minority' ('minority classification') into the Column box.
    Place dependent variable 'jobcat' ('job category') into the Row box.
    Click *Cells* → *Column percentages* → *Continue*.
    Click *Statistics*.
- Select *Chi-Square* → *Continue* → *OK*.

Following this procedure results in a table called 'Chi-Square Tests' being produced in the Output window (see Figure 23).

To interpret your results, you only need to pay attention to the first row of 'Chi-Square Tests' called 'Pearson Chi-Square'. In this row, the 'Value' column provides the calculated chi-square value (e.g., value 26.172), which is a measure of how different the observed and expected frequency tables are. The final column in this row ('Asymp. Sig. [2-sided]') provides you with the statistical significance value (e.g., sig. .000). Note that because an actual significance value is given here, you do not have to look up the critical value in a table. You just need to decide on an acceptable level of significance (p <.05, p <.01, etc.).

Figure 23 Output for Pearson chi-square

Chi-Square Tests

	Value	df	Asymp. Sig. (2-sided)
Pearson Chi-Square	26.172[a]	2	.000
Likelihood Ratio	29.436	2	.000
Linear-by-Linear Association	9.778	1	.002
N of Valid Cases	474		

[a] 0 cells (.0%) have expected count less than 5. The minimum expected count is 5.92.

T-tests

The *t-test* is a parametric test to assess the significance of a difference between means. This test is used when the dependent variable under investigation is measured on an interval/ratio level but the independent variable is not. Following from the previous example, it makes sense to expect that because we determined that minorities and non-minorities tend to have different types of jobs, their salaries will also differ. To test this idea, we could compare the mean salaries between these two groups to see whether there is a significant difference between them. The procedure for conducting this test are described below.

Procedure
- Select *Analyze* from the menu.
- Select *Compare Means → Independent Samples T-Test*.
    Move dependent variable 'salary' (current salary) into the Test Variable(s) box.
    Move independent variable 'minority' (minority classification) into the Grouping Variable box.
    Click *Define Groups* to specify the values for the two groups that you want to compare.
    In our case, we want to compare minorities and non-minorities, so we enter '0' under 'Group 1' and '1' under 'Group 2'.
- Click *Conti → OK*.

The procedures for generating a t-test are illustrated in Figure 24.

Figure 24 Requesting a t-test

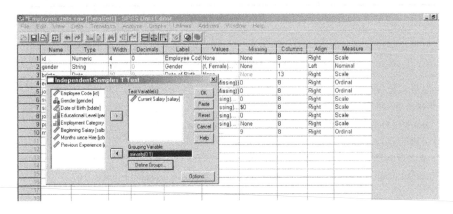

Following this procedure, two tables will appear in the Output window (Figure 25). The first table is titled 'Group Statistics'. Looking in the column 'Mean', you will observe that non-minorities in your sample had an average salary of $36,023, while the minorities had an average salary of $28,714 (a difference of about $7300). The results suggest that there are minority/non-minority differences in annual salary.

Is this difference statistically significant? Or is it probably a result of sampling error? To answer this question, look in the table titled 'Independent Samples Test' and the first row in the column 'Sig. (2-tailed)'. This is your significance value (in this example, .000), which is ready for interpretation.

Figure 25 Output of t-test

Group statistics					
	minority Minority Classification	N	Mean	Std. Deviation	Std. Error Mean
salary Current Salary	0 No	370	36023.31	18044.096	938.068
	1 Yes	104	28713.94	11421.638	1119.984

Independent Samples Test										
		Levene's Test for Equality of Variances		t-test for Equality of Means						
									95% Confidence Interval of the Difference	
		F	Sig.	t	df	Sig. (2-tailed)	Mean Difference	Std. Error Difference	Lower	Upper
salary Current Salary	Equal variances assumed	28.487	.000	3.915	472	.000	7309.369	1867.111	3640.491	10978.246
	Equal variances not assumed			5.003	262.188	.000	7309.369	1460.936	4432.707	10186.030

Section 10: Sampling Distributions and Sample Size

SPSS allows you to draw random samples of cases from your data set. The following instructions explain the procedures for this task.

Drawing a random sample

In SPSS, we can take samples from our data set (i.e., a sample of a sample, so to speak) via the Select Cases procedure. There are various reasons that you might want to do so, such as reducing the size of your data file without compromising its representativeness.

Imagine that you have a data set including a very large sample of several hundred thousand cases. Working with such a large sample may be awkward, so you plan to take a random sub-sample of these cases that will give you a much more manageable sample size. If you employ random sampling techniques, it is likely that your sub-sample will closely resemble the full sample. In any case, you can check this outcome by running frequencies of key variables for the full sample and comparing them with frequencies for the sub-sample.

The example below illustrates the procedure for this task, but for the sake of illustration, a random sample of cases from a comparably smaller file is used.

Step 1: Use the Select Cases procedure to select your random sub-sample (Figure 26)
- In the Data Editor window, go to *Data* menu → *elect Cases*.
- Select *Random Sample of Cases*.
     Click Sample box.
     Enter the percentage of cases that you would like (in this case, 20 per cent was used).
- Select *Continue* and *OK*.

Figure 26 Selecting a random sample of cases

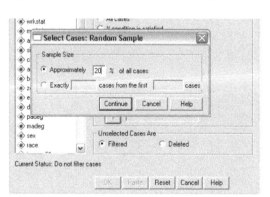

Step 2: Run a frequency distribution of any variable to check your procedure

To check the accuracy of your sub-sample sample result, run a frequency distribution for any variable, and look at the number of cases. The sample size of your sub-sample should be very near (subject to rounding error) to the original size times the percentage you selected. This test will confirm that you selected the sample correctly.

Having confirmed the accuracy of your procedure, you can check on the accuracy of the results. Toward this end, run frequency distributions of selected socio-demographic variables (gender, age, education, and so on) in both the original data set and the selected data set. Compare these outcomes, and see how closely the sample selection approximates the original distribution.

Step 3: Return to the original sample

To remove the 'Select If' filter that produced the selected sample and return to the original data set, complete the following steps: *Data* menu → *Select Cases* → *Select All Cases* and *OK*. Once you have completed this routine, delete 'filter_$' found in your data set by highlighting the column and pressing delete.

SPSS Quick Reference Guide

This guide covers the SPSS procedures you will use most often in the lab.

How do I . . .

Run a frequency distribution?

- From the menu bar, select *Analyze → Descriptive Statistics → Frequencies.*
- In left-hand box, scroll and highlight your variable name and press *Run* button.(◀)
- Select *OK* to execute the *Frequency* command.

Run a bivariate crosstabulation?

- Select *Analyze* from the menu bar.
- Select *Descriptive Statistics → Crosstabs.*
  Move dependent variable to Row box.
  Move independent variable to Column box.
- Select *Cells → select Column Percentages → select Continue → OK.*

Select cases by a condition?

- In the Data Editor window, go to *Data* menu → *Select Cases.*
- Select *If condition is satisfied →* Click If box.
  Scroll and highlight target variable in left box.
  Press arrow button.
  Select condition: for example = (equal to) and '1' (the value for married people).
- Select *Continue* and *OK.*

Recode a variable?

- Go to *Transform* menu → *Recode → Into Different Variables.*
- Select variable from list of variables and move it into the Input Variable box.
  Select a name for your new variable and type it into the Output Variable box.
  Click on *Change* button.
  Select *Old and New Values* button.
  Select first *Range* button under *Old Value* dialogue box, and enter into the boxes the lowest and highest values in the range of values you want grouped. Enter the value '1' in the New Value box. Click on *Add.* Repeat for all of the desired categories.
  When finished recoding, select *Continue* and choose *OK.*
- Always run a frequency distribution of your new variable and compare its percentages with your original one to make sure that it was recoded correctly, including the exclusion of missing values (if applicable).

Notes

'You Play the Way You Practice': A Preface for Students

[1] As contrasted with the all-too-prevalent disingenuous forms.

Lab 2

[1] Barry Schwartz. 2004. *The Paradox of Choice: Why Less Is More*. New York: Harper Perennial.

[2] This translation from talk to observation is done through the use of *operational definitions*. See Lab 3 of our 2009 companion volume, *The Methods Coach*, for a review of the connection between conceptual and operational definitions.

[3] Levels of measurement are discussed in Lab 4 of our 2009 companion volume *The Methods Coach*.

[4] This list is not exhaustive and does not include, for example, interquartile range or index of qualitative variation.

Lab 4

[1] Source: www.statcan.ca/English/census01/Info/collection.cfm.

[2] The Census is targeted at every individual living in Canada. Therefore, it is not a sample per se but rather a complete enumeration of the Canadian population. As a result, the number of cases in the public-use micro-data file provided by Statistics Canada is very large. For current purposes, a random sample of that huge file has been selected in a way that resembles the complete data set very closely in terms of key socio-demographic characteristics.

[3] Source: www.statcan.ca/english/census01/Products/Reference/dict/hou019.htm.

Lab 5

[1] Statistics Canada defines a household as 'a person or group of persons (other than foreign residents) who occupy the same dwelling and do not have a usual place of residence elsewhere in Canada' (www12.statcan.ca/english/census01/Products/Reference/dict/hou009.htm).

Lab 6

[1] You might notice that you have a lot of missing cases in your crosstabulation. This is because SPSS will automatically omit respondents who were not asked the question on willingness to live common-law, so you can safely ignore them.

Lab 8

[1] This variable excludes parents who do not work for pay; that is not a problem.

[2] This variable excludes parents who do not do any child care; that is not a problem.

[3]Please note: The examples of social science variables—and relationships between them—that are typically used in textbooks tend to be far more 'perfect' than real-life social science variables. In other words, at times you will need to use your judgment and look for *approximate* meeting of requirements and assumptions for correlation.

Lab 9

[1]Nelson Mandela. 1994. *The Long Walk to Freedom*. New York: Little Brown.

Lab 11

[1]Statistics Canada, www12.statcan.ca/english/census01.

[2]According to Donna Dasko, senior vice-president, Environics Research Group, 'One question on an omnibus poll of 2,000 people can cost $1,500.' (CBC. 2006. 'Voter toolkit: Polling FAQs'. www.cbc.ca/canadavotes/voterstoolkit/pollfaqs.html.)

SPSS Essentials

[1]Consult the SPSS website for an extensive roster (www.spss.com).

[2]Our students find the following volume helpful: Darren George and Paul Mallery. 2008. *SPSS for Windows Step by Step: A Simple Guide and Reference*. Boston: Pearson.

[3]The student version of SPSS is just a stripped-down version of the software. It can analyze fewer cases and is less sophisticated but is certainly adequate for current purposes.

[4]Note that the value of R^2 is quite low. We can surmise that this is because we need to take into account additional factors that influence how many children a person has, such as their age (i.e., they may still be young and have not had all of their children yet). We could add more variables to our analysis (i.e., do a multivariate regression adding variables like age) to look at the influence of such factors.

About the Authors

Lance W. Roberts is a professor in the Sociology Department and a fellow of St John's College at the University of Manitoba. He recently completed a term as scientific director of the Winnipeg Area Study, a survey research unit. For more than three decades, he has taught undergraduate and graduate methods and statistics courses and is the author of several books and dozens of articles on social trends, ethnic relations, education, and inequality.

Karen Kampen is a doctoral candidate in the Sociology Department's PhD program at the University of Manitoba, where she holds the position of lab instructor. Her main areas of interest are environmental sociology and research methods. She has spent 15 years working in universities as a research associate, collecting and analyzing data for long-term projects such as a health care program evaluation and books on social trends and poverty. She also serves as an instructor for introductory sociology and undergraduate methods courses.

Tracey Peter is an assistant professor in the Sociology Department at the University of Manitoba. Her areas of specialization include data analysis and syntax programming, skills she advanced during her tenure as a research associate and programming manager with a nationally based evaluation research company. Professor Peter currently teaches undergraduate and graduate courses in research methods and statistics and is working on several projects in mental health and violence, suicide prevention, education, and immigration research.

Index

Page numbers in **bold font** indicate applications.